For Melissa
thank you!

AN

HONOURABLE

MAN

BY

MICHAEL MCMANUS

Much love

Michael

Michael McManus :)

Published by Playdead Press 2018

© Michael McManus 2018

Michael McManus has asserted his rights under the
Copyright, Design and Patents Act, 1988, to be
identified as the author of this work.

A CIP catalogue record for this book is available from
the British Library.

ISBN 978-1-910067-72-7

Playdead Press
www.playdeadpress.com

The first full production of *An Honourable Man* ran from 20 November to 8 December 2018 at the White Bear Theatre, jointly presented by An Honourable Man Productions and the White Bear Theatre. The cast and creatives were as follows:

CAST

Timothy Harker	JOE NEWMAN
Lisa Bowerman	ANNE
Max Keeble	SAM
Thomas Mahy	JOSH AND PR MAN
Dee Sadler	LIZ
Annie Tyson	MAGGIE

CREATIVES

Jolley Gosnold	DIRECTOR
Claude Baskind	ASSOCIATE DIRECTOR
Mike Lees	SET AND COSTUME DESIGN
Joseph Ed Thomas	LIGHTING DESIGN
Steve Broster	A/V DIRECTOR & PRODUCER
Will Gosnold	SOUND DESIGNER
Fred Kelly	STAGE & TECH MANAGER

Additional performers (in the pre-recorded audio-visual sections of the play) in the premiere run at the White Bear Theatre included:

Sandy Barton, Sue Cameron, Lord (Michael) Cashman, Rt Hon Kenneth Clarke QC MP, Professor Sir John Curtice, Nigel Evans MP, Mark Foster, Shaun Ley, Michael McManus, James Naughtie, Su Pollard, Carolyn Quinn, Sakuntala Ramanee, Mark Reynolds, Simon Stallard, Stephen Thorne.

MICHAEL MCMANUS | WRITER

Michael has been in and around politics for far too long. He has worked for three Prime Ministers and as a special adviser in three Government departments. He has also been a parliamentary candidate and a finalist in a number of parliamentary selections. He was the last executive director of the old Press Complaints Commission and, with the then chair David Hunt, managed its transition into the new Independent Press Standards Organisation (IPSO). For over a decade he was the Westminster political diarist for the *Sunday Post* newspaper and he is the author and/or editor of a number of books. His biography of Jo Grimond (*Towards the Sound of Gunfire*, Birlinn, 2001) and his account of the Conservative Party's approach to LGBT rights (*Tory Pride and Prejudice*, Biteback, 2011, but sadly out of print and definitely due for a revised and updated edition) are arguably his most scholarly tomes, but his booze-stained magnum opus with (and about) his great friend the wonderful and much missed actor Nicholas Courtney (*Still Getting Away With It*, scificollector.co.uk, 2005) is much his most personal – and probably his favourite. His account of the life of Sir Edward Heath, *Edward Heath: A Singular Life* (Elliott & Thompson, 2016) was widely praised and nominated as "Book of the Week" in the *Daily Mail* – an accolade which would have appalled Sir Edward, but one that brought a wide smile to the face of the author. With co-writer Charlie Ross Mackenzie, music director Matt Malone and director Bryan Hodgson, Michael has also been working on *Tainted*, a new musical featuring the songs of Marc Almond and Soft Cell, which had a successful showcase at The Vaults in London, in October 2018.

JOLLEY GOSNOLD | DIRECTOR

Jolley is a writer and director for both stage and screen. He is based in London, where he completed a 4-year integrated BA/MA in Directing at Drama Centre London (CSM). He was awarded the 2016 Lilian Baylis Award, which recognises promising talent from UK drama schools; and was also a recipient of the Leverhulme Bursary. In 2017 he co-directed *The Prophetic Visions of Bethany Lewis* for Edinburgh Fringe, which won the Brighton Fringe Award for Excellence. Jolley was also the Founding Chief Executive and Artistic Director of Global English Theatre, an international theatre-in-education company. Jolley's other directing credits include *The Infinity Mirror* (Here Now Ensemble), *To the Passer-by / Just do right* (Atramental Theatre), *Goodnight Macbeth* (Plesion). Assistant directing credits include *Hamlet* (Octagon Theatre, Bolton) and *The Caucasian Chalk Circle* (Platform Theatre). He is currently developing a number of projects, including his debut feature film in collaboration with Room One Films and a new stage production of Henrik Ibsen's *An Enemy of the People* with Here Now Ensemble.

CLAUDE BASKIND | ASSOCIATE DIRECTOR

Claude is a London-based writer and director. In 2017, he completed an MA in screen directing at the Drama Centre London. His short film, *Alright Harry?* Screened in competition at the 2017 London Short Film Festival. He has worked as an assistant director and freelance script reader. He has been, at different times, a corporate lawyer, delivery driver and pearl fisherman.

STEVE BROSTER | AV DIRECTOR AND PRODUCER

Steve is a self-shooting producer/director of some considerable resilience. He started his first film 30 years ago. He's seriously considering finishing it. Since then he's made programmes for Sky Sports and the BBC, won an international film festival award for editing – and made over 50 documentaries of varying lengths for BBC Worldwide / 2 Entertain. He's a versatile and imaginative film-maker, equally at home with serious drama, cutting-edge comedy and incisive documentary. He's currently writing and directing a full cast audio drama and making short films with the University of Birmingham.

MIKE LEES | SET AND COSTUME DESIGN

Mike has designed sets and costumes for over 200 productions throughout the UK, Europe, the Middle East and America. Recent work includes: *Salad Days* (Union Theatre, Theatre Royal Bath, & UK Tour – Offie Awards Finalist); *Privates on Parade* (Union Theatre – Offie Awards Finalist); *The Toxic Avenger* (Southwark Playhouse – Offie Awards Finalist); *The Tailor-Made Man* (White Bear Theatre – Offie Awards Finalist*); Romeo & Juliet and Undine* (Bolshoi Ballet Moscow & Yekaterinburg Ballet, Golden Mask winner 2017); *The Fairy's Kiss* (Diaghilev Festival); *Stop the Play!* (Trafalgar Studios); *Matilde* (Vaudeville Theatre*); Fred Astaire: His Daughter's Tribute* (London Palladium); *What I heard About Iraq* (Arts Theatre & UK Tour); *Gone* (New Ambassadors); *Madama Butterfly* (Hackney Empire); and *The Drowsy Chaperone* (Playhouse, New York). As a costume designer, Mike has created costumes and / or outfits for the National Theatre, the BBC, the Theatre Museum, Lady Gaga, KACTA, The X Factor series 10 & 11 and Downton Abbey.

JOSEPH ED THOMAS | LIGHTING DESIGN

Joseph trained at Arts Educational Schools London and RADA. Lighting Design Credits include: *Tainted - A New Musical*, Workshop (The Vaults, Waterloo); *Lost Boys New Town* (National Youth Theatre, The Hope Theatre); *Closets the Musical* (Hope Mill Theatre); *The 43 Club* (The Other Palace), *The Jury A New Musical* (Brindley Theatre); *Perfectly Ordinary the New Musical* (GLive Guildford); *Shakespeare's Sister* (Courtyard Theatre, Hoxton); *The Blue Electric Wind* (Bush Theatre); *Status Update* (Soho Theatre); *Drowned or Saved* (Drayton Arms Theatre); *Lobster* (Theatre 503); *Little Girl Inside Me* (ThePlace); UK Premier of *Miracle on 34th Street* (BridgeHouseSE20); *Down The Hatch* (RADA GBS Theatre); *Dogfight* (The Capitol Theatre, Horsham); *A Destiny with Death* (Cockpit Theatre); *Dominoes* (Wandsworth Fringe Festival & Tara Arts); *A New Brain* (The Angles Theatre); *La Clemenza di Tito, Lucia di Lammermoor, La Cenerentola* (Opera de Bauge 2017 rep season).
www.josephedthomas.co.uk.

FREDERICK KELLY | STAGE MANAGER

Frederick wrote and directed *Blighters*, an absurdist black comedy about the Irish Potato Famine. The film received a number of awards including an Award of Merit at the IndieFest Film Awards and an Award of Merit (Special Mention) at the Accolade Global Film Competition. Frederick was assistant director on *Marching on Together* (Old Red Lion, 2015) and work-shopped his own play, *Let the Mind Wander*, at the Tabard Theatre. He shot a music video for cult singer-songwriter, Jont, and recently finished shooting another short film, which in now in post-production.

TIMOTHY HARKER | JOE NEWMAN

Timothy came late to the acting profession, graduating from Drama Studio London in 2014. Theatre includes: *Confessional* (Southwark Playhouse); *Incident at Vichy* (Finborough); *Consumables* (King's Head and Vault Festival); *Telo* (Gielgud Theatre / RADA Festival); *Montgomery* (Hope Theatre); *A Chaste Maid In Cheapside* (Rose Playhouse). TV includes: *Peaky Blinders* (BBC / Tiger Aspect). Film includes: *The Village In The Woods* (Brake3 Productions).

LISA BOWERMAN | ANNE

Lisa trained at the Bristol Old Vic Theatre School and has worked extensively in many major theatres throughout the country, including Leicester, Bristol, Leatherhead, Plymouth, Salisbury, Harrogate, Windsor, Manchester, York and many more. Tours have included *Hay Fever, Blood Brothers* and *The Circle* for Oxford Stage Company, and, most recently, a lost J.B. Priestley play, *The Roundabout*, at The Park Theatre, London and had a run as part of the Brits Off Broadway season in New York. Television includes: *Casualty* (first two series as paramedic Sandra Mute), *Doctor Who* (*Survival*), *The Vision Thing, The Count of Solar, McCallum, Bad Girls, Night & Day, Doctors, Spooks, Hollyoaks* and *Coronation Street*. Lisa has recorded many plays for BBC Radios 3 & 4 and Independent Radio Drama Productions, and has for the last 20 years played the title role in the Doctor Who spin-off audio series Professor Bernice Summerfield for Big Finish Productions, as well as regular characters in their series of *Sapphire & Steel* and *Jago & Litefoot*, and many other guesting roles – most recently in *King Lear* (with David Warner). She is also a prolific audio drama director, having directed many series for Big Finish, and other companies.

MAX KEEBLE | SAM

Max graduated from Drama Centre London in 2017. Credits whilst training include: *Hedda Gabler*, *The Caucasian Chalk Circle* and *Herons*. Other credits include *Maurice* (Above the Stag), *Goodnight Macbeth* (Plesion), *Mydidae* (Wimbledon College of Arts), *The Infinity Mirror* (Here Now Ensemble), *Faithful Ruslan: A Tale of a Guard Dog* (Belgrade Theatre Coventry, Citizens Theatre Glasgow and KP Productions) and *I Run* (Cut The Cord).

THOMAS MAHY | JOSH

Thomas trained at Drama Centre London where he was awarded the Sir John Gielgud Bursary. He made his London theatre debut recently in Phillip Ridley's *Vincent River* at The Park Theatre, for which he received an Offie nomination as best male actor. In autumn 2018, he has been touring in *I Dare You*, a new play by Tom Powell (Nottingham Playhouse and Curve Leicester). Thomas was also seen recently in *Wuthering Heights*, playing Heathcliff at The Euro Theater Central, Bonn.

DEE SADLER | LIZ

Dee trained at Drama Centre London. Theatre includes: *Blue Kettle*, *The Bristol Hum*, *Sucking on the Pips*, *Far Away*, *Two Noble Kinsmen*, *My Green Your Grey*, *Shang-a-Lang* (Bristol Old Vic); *A Kind Of Alaska*, *Misery*, *Blavatsky's Tower*, *Pool Party*, *Showing the Monster*, *Egg Shell Blues* and *Metal Remains* (Theatre West); *Trojan Women*, *Breathing Corpses* (Cheltenham Everyman); *Viral Sutra* (Finborough Arms); *King Lear*, *A Midsummer Night's Dream* (Shakespeare At The Tobacco Factory); *Ghost Train*, *The Beguiled*, *Ruffian on the Stair*, *Knock Twice for Yes* and *Something for Christmas* (Angelhair Prods.); *Playhouse Creatures* and *The Country* (Milagro Prod.);

Blood Is Thicker Than Water (Butterfly Psyche); and *Three Musketeers* (Meteoric Rise Tour). Audio includes: *The Fall of the House of Abercorn* and *Unholiest Order* (Moonscape Productions). TV includes: *Peak Practice, Home Farm Twins, No Place Like Home, Travelling Man, Doctor Who, All Creatures Great and Small, Casualty, The Bill, Wycliffe, Ultraviolet* and *Pie In The Sky.*

ANNIE TYSON | MAGGIE

After graduating from Birmingham University with a degree in Drama and Theatre Arts, Annie trained at Drama Centre London. She worked as an actor in regional theatre, in plays including *Pygmalion* and *Educating Rita.* Work in London has included new music-theatre at the Old Red Lion and the King's Head, *The Enemies Within* at the Young Vic and *King Lear* at the Old Vic. Recent theatre work has included *A Streetcar Named Desire* and *Love On The Dole* (Octagon Theatre, Bolton). In July 2017, Annie appeared in *The Lizzie Play* at the RADA Festival. Her TV work includes *Juliet Bravo, Casualty, The Fourth Floor, 40, A Touch of Frost, Coronation Street, Damon and Debbie* and *Brookside.* She has also taught and directed at Drama Centre London, and continues this strand of her career at RADA. She has just contributed to a new book on contemporary actor training and is a tutor/mentor for the diversity in training initiative "Open Door."

THE WHITE BEAR THEATRE

The White Bear Theatre was founded in 1988 by Michael Kingsbury and focuses on new writing and lost classics. It exists to nurture and develop exceptional new and existing talent and offer a space where risks can be taken. Amongst those who have cut their teeth at The White Bear Theatre are Joe Penhall, Dennis Kelly, Emily Watson, Mehmet Ergen, Tamzin Outhwaite, Kwame Kwei Armah, Vicky Featherstone, Torben Betts and Lucinda Coxon. *The White Bear Theatre* has also developed and hosted work by a new generation of theatre makers including Verity Bargate Winner Vicky Jones, Blanche McIntyre, The Ugly Sisters, and Simon Evans. Former White Bear Theatre Associates include Adam Spreadbury-Marr and Box of Tricks Theatre.

The White Bear Theatre has received numerous awards including Off West End Awards in 2011 and 2012; and the Mark Marvin/Peter Brook Award for 2012/13. Other awards include Time Out Best Fringe Venue, Peter Brook Empty Space Award for Best Up and Coming Venue, Carling London Fringe Awards for Best Actor & Best Production, and the Fringe Report Award for Outstanding Achievement. Transfers have included the recent production of *Inigo* transferring to The Pleasance, *The Confessions of Gordon Brown* and *Madness in Valencia*, both to the Trafalgar Studio 2, and *Round the Horne... Revisited,* which played in the West End for 18 months, completed 3 first-class tours and was chosen for the Royal Variety Performance. The London première of John Osborne's second play *Personal Enemy* transferred to the prestigious Brits Off-Broadway Festival in New York, and other transfers include *Muswell Hill* to The Park, *The Duchess of Malfi* to the Southwark Playhouse, and *Count Oederland* to the Arcola. The recent, Offie-nominated production of *Out There on Fried Meat Ridge Road* transferred to Trafalgar 2 in May 2017.

White Bear Theatre
138 Kennington Park Road
London
SE11 4DJ

Email: info@whitebeartheatre.co.uk

Tel: 020 7793 9193

Website: www.whitebeartheatre.co.uk

Special thanks to: all the cast and creatives; Michael Kingsbury and the White Bear Theatre; the team at the White Bear Pub, Kennington; Matthew Darling and the Partners and Staff of DAC Beachcroft LLP; Elliot Robinson at Playdead Press; James Addison; Leo Austin; Catherine Bailey; Peter Batey; Tristan Beint; David Benson; Peter Bingle; Guy Black; Roly Botha; Peter Botting; Gyles Brandreth; Steve & Stella Broster; Sue Cameron; Neil Carmichael; Jane Cooper; Martin Davies & Paul Leake; Nick Denys; Michael Dobbs; Churia Emembolu; David Hale; David and Paddy Hunt; Waris Hussein; Sir Bernard and Baroness (Anne) Jenkin; Fiona Macdonald; Diane McHale; Noel McManus; Julian Mitchell; Ivan Mulcahy; Steve Norris; Mark Oosterveen; Terri Paddock; Matthew Parris; Terry Patmore; Giles Peel; Su Pollard; Stephen Pound MP; Ken Pyne; Sakuntala Ramanee; Mike Robertson; Lewis Robinson; Nicholas Robinson; Simon Stallard; Stephen Thorne; Will Timmins; Polly Toynbee.

For Georgina, who told me to make sure it happened –
which is probably why it did – with love

SCENE 1

DARKNESS AND V/O

A VOICE   Now we ask you, please, to look forward. Just in time I mean. It's not like there's actually anything to look forward to. I'm not daft. I mean, have you seen the news today? [Sighs]. I haven't. I pre-recorded this a month ago. (Beat). But even so I can feel pretty confident it won't be a barrel of laughs. Anyway, forward we go, perhaps to 2022 or 2021, or even a "2020 vision". A time when Brexit has happened. Well, sort of. You know. A bit. Ish. (Beat). And we keep having elections too, but no one ever wins. So nothing really changes. Trains are cancelled, factories close, the High Streets carry on dying, the NHS has its annual winter crisis, and luxury flats lie fallow while desperate families remain homeless. It's wrong isn't it? But the political parties just bumble along regardless, like squabbling families clinging together out of habit, or fear. Certainly not mutual love. Mutual loathing, more like. It's time for a new party, everyone keeps saying. Break the mould of British politics! Well, be careful what you wish for...

SCENE 2

AN EMPTY ROOM

The screen springs to life.

V/O   The result was announced just a few moments
                   ago.

Candidates lined up behind the returning officer.

R. OFFICER   I therefore declare that Joseph James
                   Newman has been duly elected as the Member
                   of Parliament for Teesside Central.

A television studio. One of the guests is visibly astonished.

OBSERVER   An incredible result. This part of Teesside has
                   been held by Labour since the 1930s and the
                   party has now lost it, not to the
                   Conservatives, not to a Liberal, but to an
                   independent.

PRESENTER   Well, to the incumbent Labour MP, standing
                   as "Independent Labour"/

OBSERVER   Nonetheless, this is probably the most
                   striking personal triumph for an independent
                   candidate since Dick Taverne in Lincoln in
                   1973/

V/O   Mr. Newman is now addressing the crowd
                   gathered outside the count.

As the result ["Joe Newman holds Teesside Central with a
majority of just over 7,000 - winning 51 per cent of the vote"] is

17

shown across the bottom of the screen, JOE is seen making an acceptance speech, struggling to be heard.

JOE (*On screen*) Thanks to the wonderful people of this great constituency, this is truly a momentous day. It was predicted by no one. Not even by me. (*Raucous laughter and cheers*). This victory belongs to everybody, to everybody who helped and everybody who voted for me. This is a victory for decency, for independence of mind and also for integrity in public life. Thank you all, from the bottom of my heart.

A great cheer goes up. A V switches channel.

PRESENTER Newly independent candidate Joe Newman has won a dramatic victory in the by-election at Teesside Central tonight. The well-publicised attempt to oust him from Westminster, by deselecting him as a Labour candidate, seems to have spectacularly backfired. Here's what Mr Newman had to say in his acceptance speech - and, as you'll see, some of his opponents were none too pleased.

SCREEN off. JOE, SAM, LIZ and ANNE tumble into the room.

SAM Unbelievable. It's unbelievable.

ANNE Your majority actually went up at a by election.

SAM   17,000 votes. Fuck me. I mean, not literally.
               Not now. Not in here. The floor is filthy and
               that sofa might collapse. But fuck me.

They laugh.

JOE   Well I know I have to keep saying it's a
               historic victory that could change everything.
               But you know what? It may be precisely that.

LIZ   You did it. You actually did it.

JOE   I know. What the Hell do I do now?

SAM   We can think about that tomorrow.

SCENE 3

THE WESTMINSTER OFFICE.

ANNE and SAM are surveying a vast mound of unopened post.

SAM   Ach, Anne, you're like a hundred years old
              anyway. None of this matters to you. You can
              just go and retire to a fossil park or
              something. This is my first job. I only left uni
              nine months ago.

ANNE   You're behaving like your balls only dropped
              nine months ago. Do your job. The one you
              signed up to do/

SAM   You're telling me we're coping?

ANNE   I know you always have more important
              matters to attend to/

SAM   I do, so. I have to get loads of briefs done.

ANNE   More like briefs down. Even during the by-
              election campaign you couldn't keep your
              trousers on/

SAM   All those young, innocent, athletic
              volunteers. No one knew what to do with
              them, as the nights drew in.

ANNE   You certainly knew what to do with one of
              them.

SAM   Just one, say you? How very dare you? Three
              it was. Two at the same time.

ANNE	I honestly don't need to know/
SAM	In mitigation, think of those cold, lonely dark nights, hundreds of miles from home/
ANNE	You had a duty of care/
SAM	I did more than care for them. An entire army of political virgins on the march/
ANNE	Not virgins for long. You couldn't keep your trousers on if they were welded to your legs. We should have your penis tasered.
SAM	Er, can we not discuss my penis, please?
ANNE	Fine by me. It's not a big preoccupation of mine. Not a big anything really.
SAM	You're a witch.
ANNE	I'm your fairy godmother.
SAM	I'm not your fairy.

JOE enters.

JOE	Morning Anne, Sam. What news?
SAM	Anne has taken up lecturing.
JOE	I said "news"/
ANNE	A few home truths, that's all.
JOE	Everything alright?

ANNE and SAM say nothing; they just catch one another's eye.

	Anyone?
ANNE	We can't go on like this.
JOE	It's exciting.
SAM	It's not exciting.
ANNE	We have thousands of unanswered letters. Thousands.
SAM	And there's hundreds of e-mails coming through every hour. They're getting automated responses, but that's all we can manage.
ANNE	A lot of the letters have donations in them. Cash/
SAM	Or/
ANNE	Cheques.
SAM	Yeah, cheques. What the Hell are they?
JOE	Thanks for making me feel old.
SAM	You are old. Actually, what's cash?
JOE	Yes, very good. Listen, everyone deserves a proper acknowledgement.
ANNE	Joe, there's just two of us.
JOE	People are sending money?
SAM	Sixty grand and counting.

JOE	Well, there's the answer. We can afford extra help.
ANNE	That's all very well. But what do we say to all these people? What's the great plan?
JOE	Well, I do seem to have captured the public imagination somewhat/
SAM	[*OTT*] Dead on you have. But perhaps if they could see this scene of chaos, horror and despair...
JOE	How many are constituents?
ANNE	Well, some. I don't know. Some.
JOE	What are they saying?
ANNE	They're generally happy/
SAM	Apart from the Labour members.
JOE	Oh.
SAM	They say you should have stayed to fight, that you could have/
JOE	I did fight. I fought those bastards every inch of the way, but they infiltrated the entire organisation, from top to bottom.

SAM gurns. ANNE groans.

First the trade unions, then the party branches. I didn't want to hurt the Labour Party. I wanted to help save it.

SAM	Wind your neck in. What's done is done.
ANNE	Joe, could we have a word, please?
JOE	Of course.
ANNE	A private word?

SAM shrugs.

SAM	I'll carry on yomping across the European letter mountain.
ANNE	Joe, you know I like to keep my ear to the grapevine?
JOE	No one at Westminster talks to me anymore, apart from the policemen, the postmen and the catering staff.
ANNE	They're the nicest people here.
JOE	They're being nicer than ever.
ANNE	The secretaries of Westminster have been beating a path to my door.
JOE	We can't give them all jobs.
ANNE	It's not them I want to discuss.
JOE	Oh?
ANNE	It's the MPs who employ them.
JOE	And?
ANNE	There's at least ten you should talk to. Urgently. Maybe twenty.

JOE   What about?

ANNE   You might not remain in splendid isolation
                 for long.

JOE   How so?

ANNE   People are starting to look to you.

JOE   Look to me? For what?

ANNE   A lead.

JOE   A lead?

ANNE   Well, for now, all I need is your permission/

JOE   That's never concerned you before/

ANNE   To   encourage   this.   To   have   these
                 conversations.

JOE   Don't trust anyone.

ANNE   I never have.

JOE   Not even me?

ANNE   You don't want to know the answer to that
                 question.

JOE   What about Sam?

ANNE   Trust Sam?

They both laugh.

JOE   Let's not enter the realms of fantasy. I do
                 trust his ambition, though.

ANNE	When ships sink, you don't get to choose who's in the lifeboat with you. What happens next depends on the qualities of the captain.
JOE	Assuming there's a captain on board.
ANNE	Oh I think there is.
JOE	You have my full authority. Clear my diary and get some of them in to see me. Here, wherever. My flat?
ANNE	I'd suggest your club.
JOE	What, the actors' club?
ANNE	Precisely. No one there will recognise them.
JOE	No one there recognises me. And I've been a member for years. It's like walking back into the 1950s.
ANNE	Perhaps that's what the nation's looking for. In some respects.
JOE	Anne/
ANNE	Hmmm?
JOE	Thank you. I'm impressed.
ANNE	I haven't started yet.

SCENE 4

A TELEVISION STUDIO

INTERVIEWER So, Josh Phillips, you initiated the Momentum campaign to have Joe Newman deselected/

JOSH There wasn't a campaign. There didn't need to be. There was a lot of disaffection at the grassroots/

INTERVIEWER But you did give interviews saying it was time for Mr Newman to go/

JOSH I was only saying what thousands of other people were saying, that he was a parliamentary bed-blocker whose time was up/

INTERVIEWER Well that all backfired pretty spectacularly, didn't it?

JOSH I regret nothing. Joe Newman may have got away with this for now, but/

INTERVIEWER You and Mr Newman used to be friends, though, I think?

JOSH I'm sorry?

INTERVIEWER You campaigned alongside him?

JOSH Well, yes.

INTERVIEWER So you must have been close to him.

27

JOSH   Yes. No. Not exactly. Maybe for a time. I was young. It was a mistake.

INTERVIEWER You seem upset?

JOSH   Upset? No. No. Just these questions seem so/

INTERVIEWER Intrusive?

JOSH   Stupid.

INTERVIEWER So you have no regrets?

JOSH   For standing by my principles, for trying to bring about real change? No, absolutely not. I would do it all again.

INTERVIEWER Fighting words there, from a very disappointed young campaigner. Josh Phillips, thank you very much.

SCENE 5

THE WESTMINSTER OFFICE.

JOE alone, on his mobile telephone.

JOE Yes, of course I appreciate how busy you are as Labour's esteemed chief whip. (*Beat*). Oh come on. What would people say if I came crawling back now, with my tail between my legs? (*Beat*). My place in the history books? Is that what you think this is about? (*Beat*). Alright, I'll think about it.

SAM enters. JOE is not pleased at this.

Yes, seriously. (*Beat*). Yes. (*Beat*). Yes, Soon. (*Beat*). Yes. Thank you. Bye.

JOE ends the call.

SAM Everything OK?

JOE Hmm? Yeah. Just the dry cleaner. I've had some stuff waiting there for ages.

SAM I'll collect it for you?

JOE No, no. It's fine. Don't worry.

SAM So, did you watch that interview with young Mr Phillips?

JOE Mmmm? Yes, yes I think so.

SAM I thought he was going to burst into tears. Soft little bastard.

JOE	Don't be so cruel.
SAM	Cruel? Wasn't he the cruel one?
JOE	He just did what he thought was right. He's a very earnest, serious young man, but he'll grow up/
SAM	Oh no. I knew it.
JOE	What?
SAM	You fancy him.
JOE	I do not.
SAM	You so do. Ha ha ha. Joe and Joshy sitting in a tree/
JOE	It's not funny, Sam. You know what he did to me.
SAM	OK, OK. Just having a little josh.
JOE	That'll do. Enough. (*Beat*). Are you free this evening, by any chance?
SAM	Yeah. Yeah, sure. I could be.
JOE	Could you come round to my flat? Say, around 7.30?
SAM	Really?
JOE	Yes.
SAM	Sound.

JOE   I didn't want to ask you in front of Anne. (*Beat*). Jealous.

SAM   Oh. I see. I think I see. Yes, of course. I'll be there. 7.30.

JOE   Thank you. I appreciate that. I'm finding things a bit, well/

SAM   I understand. So, I'll see you later then. Your place. At 7.30.

JOE   Yes. I'll get a nice bottle of wine. Or two. See you then.

SCENE 6

A V

PRESENTER   There is gossip at Westminster that Joe Newman may already be making overtures to Labour, in the hope of having the party whip restored.

JOE   I don't know where these rumours come from. Well, I do know where they come from, but let me tell you, there isn't a grain of truth...

SCENE 7

JOE'S LONDON FLAT.

In essence, a bed-sit – small and simple. He is sprawled on the sofa, his shirt loosened. The doorbell rings. Once, twice, insistently. He rouses himself slowly, winces at himself in the mirror, sees the time and rushes to the door. He pauses, fiddles with his shirt, tidies the sofa slightly. It is JOSH. He is holding a bottle.

JOSH   Hello.

JOE   Hello. Er…

JOSH   You seem surprised.

JOE   Well, yes. I am surprised.

JOSH   Of course you're surprised. Why am I surprised you're surprised?

JOE   This conversation could shortly disappear up its own arsehole.

JOSH   Yes. I'm sorry. I thought we should/

JOE   Talk?

JOSH   Yes.

JOE   A little late for that?

JOSH   It's not even 7.30.

JOE   That's not/

JOSH	Sorry, I see what you mean. I'm being stupid. (*Tiny beat*). I brought a bottle. (*Tiny beat*). Your favourite.
JOE	Oh.
JOSH	Yes. Oregon Pinot Noir. It's a bitch to find, but it's worth it. You taught me all about that/
JOE	Josh, it's not a good time.
JOSH	Will there ever be a good time? Joe, I just wanted to say, I/
JOE	Stop there. Just stop/
JOSH	It's not too late for us to sort things out. To start over/
JOE	Oh I think it is. Way too late. You did everything you could to fuck up my career/
JOSH	You know perfectly well/
JOE	You and your bloody rentamob/
JOSH	I don't rent them. They believe passionately in what they're doing/
JOE	That scarcely makes it better/
JOSH	You can't make an omelette without breaking eggs/
JOE	Why break the eggs if the omelette just makes people want to vomit?

JOSH	Are we truly so very different, you and I?
JOE	Oh, yes, I think we are.
JOSH	Don't you believe in equality?
JOE	Equal opportunities, yes. And a more equal society/
JOSH	Achieved by what means?
JOE	Through laws. Through progressive taxation. Through a more equal/
JOSH	More equal ownership of the means of production?
JOE	Well I suppose so, yes, but/
JOSH	And how would you achieve that?
JOE	Not by force.
JOSH	And you think we would?
JOE	Yes, yes I do - and once you start down that track/
JOSH	"You're halfway to gulags and pogroms and a police state".
JOE	Well, yes, perhaps you are.
JOSH	So democratic socialism is just a gateway drug to dictatorship?

Trying to put your opponent into a false position, are we? How infantile. How immature/

JOSH So you tell me, how do we persuade people of wealth and influence to share their privileges?

JOE You're being facetious.

JOSH I'm being realistic. Should we invite them to high tea at Fortnum's, to ask them, ever so nicely/

JOE Oh, here we go/

JOSH Yes, here we go. If they wouldn't mind so terribly much, just sharing half of a quarter of one per cent of the massive pile they inherited/

JOE What then? Hmmmm? Show trials? Line up the aristos against the wall?

JOSH We have to take the initiative.

JOE My father and I had to go on the run from people like you. You don't want to end human suffering/

JOSH Oh I don't? I had no idea/

JOE No, you just want different people to suffer. It's all about anger and envy isn't it?

JOSH Not envy. Justice. And for millions of people, it's about survival.

JOE	Taking people's property from them by diktat. Justice?
JOSH	It's called socialism. Were you ever a socialist?
JOE	I'm a democrat.
JOSH	I didn't come for this.

JOSH moves towards JOE, who pushes him away.

JOE	Josh, please...

JOE pushes JOSH away again, more vigorously this time.

	Listen. I won't/
JOSH	So masterful. If arguments fail, there's always violence.
JOE	You should know about that.
JOSH	Sorry? I'm a pacifist.
JOE	But plenty of your heroes aren't. Plastic bullets. Rubber truncheons.
JOSH	Rubber truncheons? There is a tap on the door frame. **SAM** appears.
SAM	Sorry. Am I intruding?

JOSH bridles, then calms himself. He studies SAM.

JOSH	Yes, actually.
JOE	No you aren't.

JOSH	Aren't you going to introduce us?
SAM	We've met already.
JOSH	Have we?
SAM	Several times.
JOSH	I don't recall/
SAM	You do my fecking head in, so you do. Always talkin' out your hoop/
JOSH	Hoop?
SAM	Yeah. Hoop. Yer hole. You use it well enough – and it's had more visitors than the Grand Canyon.
JOSH	Quaint.
SAM	Oh, quaint is it? I should lamp you, you stuck-up twat.
JOE	Sam. Enough.
SAM	[*TO JOSH*] I'd never forget you, even if I tried. Vacuous face, cheap shoes, heaps of ambition. Open all night and an arse like the Somme. Time for you to go, I think.
JOSH	No need to pop your dear little cork. No need at all. (*Now to JOE*). I'll be in touch.
JOE	Don't be. It's over. It's all over.
JOSH	I know when I'm not wanted.

SAM	If you knew that, you'd fuck off and die.
JOSH	Charmed. Such a silver tongue. Be careful where you put it. It might stain easily.

JOSH exits. A moment's silence.

JOE	Sorry about that.
SAM	What the Hell was he doing here?
JOE	Don't worry about him.
SAM	I brought a bottle.
JOE	Thanks. We can drink it afterwards. (*Beat*). Look, just sort yourself out in here, and I'll sort myself out in there. Won't be a minute.

JOE leaves the room. SAM puts down his bag and unwraps the bottle he has brought. It's identical to the one JOSH brought. Flustered, he thinks, hard, for a moment. Then he kicks off his shoes and begins to undress.

SAM	I'm almost ready.
JOE	Yes, yes, so am I.

JOE re-enters, holding some paperwork. A moment's stunned silence.

SAM	Oh.
JOE	You're.
SAM	You're not.
JOE	No.

SAM	Awkward.
JOE	Yes.
SAM	Isn't this. (*Beat*) Isn't this why you asked me here?

JOE cannot help himself. He stares at SAM, up and down.

JOE	Um. No. No. I wanted to discuss some constituency casework. (*Beat*). Are you trying to seduce me?
SAM	Whatever gave you that impression? (*Beat*). Well, this is embarrassing.
JOE	No, no, it's fine. We're (*beat*), we're fine. We know each other well enough.
SAM	Bit of a wasted effort then? You're sure, now? Since I'm here and/
JOE	In for a penny?
SAM	In for a pounding?

SAM begins to get dressed again.

JOE	Perhaps you'd better.
SAM	Yes?
JOE	Yes, you should. (*Beat*). I never realised you/
SAM	Well, neither did I.

JOE   Yes, best you go. We can discuss this. Not this. We can discuss things in the morning. In the office. This. This never happened.

SAM   I'll be seeing you then.

SAM exits. JOE cannot help looking pleased with himself.

SCENE 8

AV INSERT (V. short, to cover scene change)

PRESENTER   There was more rioting last night in the West Midlands, for the third night running, as protesters sought to prevent work on a luxury housing development on the outskirts of Birmingham. The Prime Minister called for calm and reiterated her view that companies and workers should be allowed to go about their lawful business without hindrance...

SCENE 9

THE WESTMINSTER OFFICE

The next morning. ANNE sits, alone. JOE enters.

ANNE	You're up bright and early.
JOE	Hardly slept a wink. Is Sam about?
ANNE	We shan't be seeing him today.
JOE	Ah.
ANNE	You don't seem surprised?
JOE	Well, he did mention/
ANNE	A headache apparently. Migraine.

Beat. Awkward.

JOE	Any progress with these other MPs?
ANNE	Oh yes. Plenty. Something's happening, you know, but no one dares make the first move.
JOE	Scared?
ANNE	Of letting go of nurse/
JOE	For fear of finding something/
ANNE	Even/
JOE	Worse.
ANNE	Such as a P45.

JOE's mobile phone rings. JOE sees the name of the caller.

JOE   I hate this bloody thing. (*Beat*). I'd better take it. Sorry.

ANNE   Of course. Don't mind me.

JOE   Dave? Hi mate. [*To ANNE, sotto voce*]. Dave Noble. Journo. What can I do for (*Beat*). Oh I see. (*Beat*). What sort of story?

JOE looks thunderstruck. Lights fade.

SCENE 10

AV INSERT (V. short, to cover scene change)

PRESENTER   The latest monthly unemployment figures, published this morning, showed another heavy increase, this time of almost 140,000 people. There are now over 3 million people unemployed in the UK, for the first time in almost 30 years.

The Chancellor of the Exchequer blamed the increase on 'the unreasonable behaviour of the European Union'.

SCENE 11

JOE'S WESTMINSTER FLAT

Minor-key music – blues perhaps. JOE pours himself a dauntingly large whisky and sighs to himself. After a moment, there is a knock on the door. He groans, pauses, then gets up and answers. It is LIZ.

JOE	Where did you spring from?
LIZ	Same as usual. I do live directly below you.
JOE	I found that out the morning I moved in, five years/
LIZ	Six.
JOE	Five years ago. And you've been correcting me ever since.
LIZ	You look like you've shat a ghost.
JOE	You might say that. (*Beat*). I just need a bit of peace and quiet.
LIZ	I shan't stay long. (*She sits down*). Just wanted to check up on you. (*Beat*). I tried to call.
JOE	I had a bad mobile experience. So I turned it off. Drink?
LIZ	Darling, I thought you'd never ask.

JOE pours another over-sized drink.

Whoah!

JOE	Scarcely a day for half measures.
LIZ	More like triple measures.
JOE	Quite. Well, bottoms up.
LIZ	So?
JOE	So?
LIZ	So?
JOE	So what?
LIZ	Why so bloody miserable? Ten days ago you were the toast of the country. A national hero!
JOE	Please don't.
LIZ	Please don't?
JOE	Please don't stop.
LIZ	And they cut you brutally off in your political prime/
JOE	The giddy heights of junior opposition front-bench spokesman on overseas development/
LIZ	Well it was something.
JOE	In politics a long title is a sign of impotence, not importance.
LIZ	Male compensation?
JOE	The irony is, I agree with Momentum on most things.

LIZ	Bit of a closet Momentumite are we?

As JOE pours more drinks. LIZ turns off the music.

JOE	Fuck. Fuckety fuck.
LIZ	What? How do I get any sense out of you?
JOE	I'm in trouble with the press.
LIZ	They haven't discovered you're really Iain Duncan Smith?
JOE	No. And I haven't been breaking electoral law or molesting any domestic animals/
LIZ	It's beginning to sound dull.
JOE	I'm trying to be serious.
LIZ	So am I. But you're making me nervous. What is it?
Beat	
JOE	A sex thing.
LIZ	Sex? You? Sex? Really?
JOE	Sex. Ha. Yes, me. Sex. Ha ha. Whatever next? Liz, the papers are going to out me.
LIZ	Out you? You're not out?
JOE	Technically not, no.
LIZ	Technically?

JOE	Well, everyone sort of knows, I guess, but I haven't exactly shouted about it on the streets of Finborough/
LIZ	How many closets can one man be in?
JOE	My closet is bigger on the inside/
LIZ	Than on the outside. Very good. (*Beat*). Hang on. We went to Pride together. On the actual march.
JOE	Officially I was an "ally".
LIZ	An ally? You were wearing a Glee T shirt.
JOE	A wholehearted ally. Full-throated.
LIZ	Full-throated? Lucky you. That shirt had "Likes Boys" emblazoned across it.
JOE	That was satirical. Ironic.
LIZ	It was certainly ironic.
JOE	And I had sunglasses on.
LIZ	Oh!
JOE	And a hat.
LIZ	The cunning master of disguise/
JOE	Do you know just how tough it was, being an ABBA fan in the 1980s? How people laughed at Chiquitita back then? Poured scorn on Voulez-Vous?

LIZ	Such courage/
JOE	In 1979, even a reincarnated Martin Luther King wouldn't have got away with liking "I Have A Dream"/
LIZ	...and fortitude.
JOE	It made me the man I am today.
LIZ	True enough.
JOE	Before the deselection, the by- election, no one cared about me.
LIZ	I did.
JOE	You know what I mean. No one cared about this. The gay thing.
LIZ	No one cared then because no one had heard of you/
JOE	Exactly/
LIZ	And no one cares now - just because no one cares.
JOE	Well I do.
LIZ	Don't be daft. The only people who give a stuff about anyone being gay are sexually repressed happy-clappies whose online activities would make a bear blush/
JOE	That's easy for/

LIZ	Never mind gay, if they find out you're a bloody immigrant, then you'll be right up shit creek. Honestly, what is it about sex and politics, politicians and sex?
JOE	Money for Labour, they used to say, and sex for Tories. Tories don't need money, but sex/
LIZ	Both for Liberals.
JOE	They have to fill their days somehow.
LIZ	Even the job titles are filthy. Chief Whip. The Honourable Member. Black Rod. Master of the Queen's Bedchamber. So what's my favourite queen been up to in his bedchamber?
JOE	I've been a fool.
LIZ	Full marks for melodrama, but "nul points" for originality. Has someone squealed about you banging my co-star?
JOE	Good God, no. They wouldn't be interested in failed actors in a fringe theatre.
LIZ	"Failed"? You cheeky sod. He was in the same production as me.
JOE	Sorry.
LIZ	You should be.
JOE	In fairness, you don't work very often.

LIZ	You evil bitch! And here's you demanding sympathy.
JOE	[*OTT*] Begging. Not demanding.
LIZ	Strange production, that one. Shakespeare - with all the female roles taken by women and the male ones by men.
JOE	I enjoyed it.
LIZ	You enjoyed the afters too.
JOE	Oh God, here we go...
LIZ	[*Now as CLEOPATRA*]

I would I had thy inches; thou shouldst know There were a heart in Egypt.

It's a very erotic passage. (*Beat*). Not the only erotic passage you explored in that show. |
JOE	It was a mistake. Like the two of us, that one time. A mistake.
LIZ	Oh. I see. Thank you very much.
JOE	I was drunk.
LIZ	I know you were. Not your finest hour.
JOE	It was hard for me.
LIZ	Hard? That's not how I remember it.
JOE	Sorry. That all came out wrong.

LIZ	Coming out wrong seems to be your speciality.
JOE	That was the night I knew, once and for all. Me and a woman/
LIZ	You didn't know before? So I made you gay?
JOE	Oh no. Bucks Fizz got to me first. If I couldn't manage it with you, then it was inconceivable that any woman could float my boat/
LIZ	Nice deployment of flattery. Typical bloody politician.
JOE	It doesn't mean I don't love you. Or that you aren't special. (*Beat*). Ahahaha, right.

JOE

[*Now as ANTONY*]

Stay for me:
Where souls do couch on flowers,
we'll hand in hand,
And with our ... Aaah..

LIZ	And with our sprightly port/
JOE	And with our sprightly port, make the ghosts ...stare?
LIZ	Make the ghosts gaze.
JOE	Gays? 'Make the ghosts gays'? Are you sure?
LIZ	Gaze.
JOE	Yeah. Gays. Gay ghosts. In Shakespeare.

LIZ	(*Mimicking a gaze*). Gaze. Not gays.

They laugh. Their mutual affection is apparent.

	Go on then, what have you done?
JOE	Huh?
LIZ	Why are the paps sniffing around?
JOE	Oh. You know that tosser who led Momentum in Finborough?
LIZ	No. (*Beat*). Not Josh Whatsisname?
JOE	Josh Phillips.
LIZ	Oh, you never shagged him?
JOE	It wasn't meant to happen.
LIZ	Well I'm sure it wasn't, but/
JOE	It was a spur-of-the-moment thing. One minute we were at a party meeting, knocking six bells out of each other and/
LIZ	Oh, you boys/
JOE	So I invited him for a drink. A last attempt at reconciliation.

LIZ bursts out laughing. So too, after a moment's hesitation, does JOE.

LIZ	Any good?
JOE	Total frigging animal.

LIZ	Fab. At least it was worth it.
JOE	I wouldn't say that.
LIZ	And the press know about this?
JOE	Dave Noble does. A journalist. A bastard, of course, but one of the less bastardy bastards.
LIZ	"Do not please sharp fate to grace it with your sorrows: bid that welcome which comes to punish us, and we punish it, seeming to bear it lightly".
JOE	What are you on about?
LIZ	In modern English, bollocks to the lot of them. Anyway, how old is Josh?
JOE	Mid-twenties? Early twenties?
LIZ	I don't think you're the one who's going to be embarrassed.
JOE	Oh God, I'll look a right dirty old fuck, won't I? A total predator.
LIZ	Predator? Well you certainly predate him. By around three decades.

LIZ kisses JOE gently.

You'll be fine. And Joe?

JOE	Hmm?
LIZ	Please, do stop swearing all the time. Potty-mouthed little twat-flap. See you, shagger.

LIZ exits. JOE picks up his mobile phone, dials, waits.

JOE　　　　　　[*Leaving a Voicemail*]. Dave, mate, hi, it's Joe Newman. Sorry to miss you. Do call back whenever it suits and of course I'll give you a comment. Cheers.

JOE sighs, drains his glass and smiles. Lights down.

SCENE 12

AV

PRESENTER   Just ten days after Joe Newman's unexpected triumph in the Teesside by-election, a Sunday newspaper has revealed details of a sexual relationship he apparently enjoyed with the young party activist responsible for driving him out of the Labour Party. There is talk of dirty tricks, although it appears, for Mr Newman at least, no publicity is bad publicity.

INTERVIEWER   Joe Newman, an opinion poll to be published tomorrow suggests 19 per cent of voters – almost one in five – now believe you'd make a good – or very good – Prime Minister.

JOE   Really?

INTERVIEWER   It's there in black and white.

JOE   Good gracious.

INTERVIEWER   You seem surprised.

JOE   Well, yes, to be candid, yes I am. Pleasantly surprised. I'm very flattered.

INTERVIEWER   Don't you have the perfect back-story for a modern politician? The ordinary bloke made good. The son of a penniless immigrant who won an Army commission, went to Cambridge, set up a school from scratch in one of the toughest towns in England/

57

JOE If you put it like that.

INTERVIEWER Perhaps you should be putting it like that too?

SCENE 13

MAGGIE'S OFFICE

JOE   I'm certain no one saw me coming in.

MAGGIE   I should hope not. I'm already next on the Momentum hit list.

JOE   They should be careful what they wish for.

MAGGIE   I was thinking. We've known each other for almost thirty years.

JOE   You've been a great mentor/

MAGGIE   Don't blame me. Anyway, these days it's more the other way around.

JOE   The chief whip's been in touch again.

MAGGIE   And?

JOE   And time is running out. She says I have one more day to decide/

MAGGIE   You're not coming back though, surely?

JOE   Well, I could sit tight as an independent/

MAGGIE   Or independent Labour/

JOE   Quite. And maybe even fight again. Possibly even win again, but ploughing on alone, without any external support or solidarity/

MAGGIE   Or/

JOE	Or I accept the party's offer to give me back the whip, pending an investigation into entryism in Teesside Central.

They look at one another and laugh.

MAGGIE	Which you believe would be undertaken to less than stringent standards of accuracy and honesty/
JOE	Which would be a total whitewash. Of course. But/
MAGGIE	But?
JOE	I was tempted, Maggie.
MAGGIE	Abasing yourself by crawling back at the first opportunity?
JOE	Quite. Which brings me to my third option.
MAGGIE	To inaugurate a new party.
JOE	People are behaving as though I already have, by standing in local by-elections for a party that doesn't exist.
MAGGIE	No.
JOE	Yes. One of them actually won.
MAGGIE	No!
JOE	Yes. A parish councillor in the West Country.
MAGGIE	Oooooh.

JOE	An uncontested election too, I grant you, but still…
MAGGIE	The law of unintended consequences. The one, ineluctable law of political life.
JOE	If the party system was a boxer, you'd say its legs had gone.
MAGGIE	Stability gives way either to chaos or to tyranny.
JOE	Meanwhile the traditional press has all but expired/
MAGGIE	So there's no one to hold the politicians to account/
JOE	Because they won't do it to each other. Leaving only social media/
MAGGIE	The breeding ground of back-bite, bullshit and bollocks.

They laugh.

JOE	Political divorces make Paul McCartney's look amicable.
MAGGIE	I've never known politics to be more poisonous. And I'm old enough to remember when Eton Mess was a pudding, not a cabinet minister or a slogan on a placard.
JOE	You were always the optimist.

MAGGIE	I'm a realist. (*Sighs*). Life used to be so much more civilised.
JOE	Manners Makyth Man?
MAGGIE	Man?
JOE	Person then.
MAGGIE	"Manners Makyth Person". Kind of kills it.
JOE	Political correctness rarely alliterates.
MAGGIE	A fine motto, though. It evokes a more honourable age.
JOE	All political careers end in failure. Didn't Enoch Powell say that?
MAGGIE	Well he would know.
JOE	The time is out of joint, but am I the man to set it right?
MAGGIE	Not more bloody Shakespeare! To be or not to be. Make up your bloody mind!
JOE	Thank you. You've answered all my questions for me.
MAGGIE	You knew all the answers before you came into this room.

SCENE 14

AV

JOE is on some kind of garish game show.

SHOW HOST   So, Joe Newman, in old English, is a kickie-wickie a disrespectful wife, an ambitious courtier or a type of bird?

JOE   I'm sure we have kickie-wickies aplenty at Westminster. [*Laughter*]. I'm going for the bird.

SHOW HOST   And we're giving you the bird, because the correct answer is a disrespectful wife.

JOE   Well, at least there's no danger of my ever having one of those [*laughter*], although some of my fellow MPs certainly can't say the same [*more laughter*]…

JOE enters the office.

It never happened. Nothing ever happened.

SAM   Jeez, OK, OK.

ANNE enters.

ANNE   Everything alright?

JOE   Why wouldn't it be?

ANNE   Just making conversation. Get out of bed the wrong side, did we?

JOE	I just didn't sleep much. I mean. I had a lot on me. On me mind. (*Beat*). Now, before the others arrive, there's something serious I need to say to both of you.
SAM	Pay rise?
ANNE	Sacking Sam?
JOE	They've offered me the whip back.
ANNE	Who did you speak to?
JOE	The chief whip. The first conversation I've ever had with her, without her braising my bollocks.
SAM	You know the old whips' credo. Get 'em by the balls and their hearts and minds will follow.
ANNE	You're never going to accept?
JOE	I told them I'd think about it.
SAM	So, threats? Moral blackmail?
JOE	Oh yes. All that and more.
ANNE	She has all the gentle courtesy of a Deliveroo driver.
JOE	And some guff about "letting the movement down". I said the only movement that concerned me was the sudden, violent one she was provoking in my bowels.

SAM	That's grand. But you still said you'd think about it?
JOE	Yes, I did. There's no going back for me, but if either of you doesn't fancy sharing my walk on the wild side, that's fine. I'll understand. No hard feelings.
SAM	No hard feelings?
JOE	Obviously, I'd miss the doubles entendres.
SAM	Aye. And is that all you'd miss?
JOE	If you aren't game for this, that's OK. I just need to know.
SAM	I feel about as special as a book endorsement from Stephen Fry.
JOE	I'd prefer you to stay. (*Beat*). Obviously.
SAM	Well I'm glad to hear that. (*Beat*). Joe, I agree with what you're doing. I admire what you're doing. You're doing the right thing.
JOE	Three different ways of making precisely the same point. We'll make a politician of you yet.
SAM	I'm insulted.
ANNE	Same for me. One hundred per cent.
JOE	Thank you both. I'm relieved.

MAGGIE and LIZ enter.

MAGGIE	Good morning.
LIZ	Hello.
MAGGIE	We slipped up the back passage.
JOE	[*Throws SAM a look*]. So. Listen, I still believe Labour did great things for this country in the past, but it's lost its way and I can't go back.
MAGGIE	Can't argue with that.
JOE	I'll never have to sing the bloody Red Flag again. (*Beat*).
	And I'll be able to sing the national anthem without feeling embarrassed.

SAM has become distracted by his mobile phone.

	Sam! Pay attention please.
SAM	Alright. Sorry. I was just looking at the latest/
JOE	This is important. Put the damned thing away.
SAM	Alright, alright. I'm turning it off. Sorry. Bloody Hell.

The others in the room are momentarily perturbed. This seemed harsh.

LIZ	So, what do you hope to achieve?
JOE	To break the Tory-Labour deadlock.

MAGGIE	Obviously.
JOE	To bring the British people back together.
ANNE	Hmmm...
JOE	To create a better, kinder and fairer society.
SAM	And on the seventh day?
JOE	I'm serious. My by-election win - sorry, our by-election win - well, it gave me a hint of something better. It's possible. I know it.
ANNE	No one likes any of the existing parties. In fact, that's been pretty much true the entire time I've been working here/
SAM	Which is a long time/
ANNE	Which is a long time, yes. And each era brings more discredit. Sleaze, cash for questions, dodgy expenses, sex scandals, Rees-Mogg-gate.
SAM	It's pronounced Smoggate.
ANNE	All that scandal and hypocrisy – it's no wonder so much voting is negative in this country – against people you despise, not for people you like or trust.
SAM	Meanwhile millions of people are still suffering the after effects of an economic crash that happened over 10 years ago/

MAGGIE	And party loyalties melt away, supplanted by personality cults.
LIZ	Sorry?
SAM	CuLts? With an "l"? Are you sure?
JOE	Well…
MAGGIE	Do you want to replace Labour?
LIZ	By which you mean, destroy it?
JOE	Listen, I'm a man of the Left. Always have been, always will be/
MAGGIE	The Left forced you out.
JOE	That doesn't mean everything they do is wrong. I admire their energy, their commitment, their sense of anger, even their ideas/
SAM	Their members.
JOE	Fuck off, Sam.
MAGGIE	If you're so keen on them, why did they target you like that?
LIZ	Perhaps you're just too old for them.
SAM	Well we know that's not true.
LIZ	Oh yes. We do now. Sorry.

JOE   And you're supposed to be my friends. God
                 help me. Liz, you came and helped in the by-
                 election. What impression did you get?

LIZ   For the first time, I understood why working-
                 class people voted for Brexit. I couldn't
                 believe people still lived like that. It's like a
                 developing country, only with running water.
                 (*Beat*). Even the water comes from a French
                 company.

ANNE   Last year, they used the old bus station in
                 Finborough in a film about a zombie
                 apocalypse.

MAGGIE   You're joking?

ANNE   Not at all. It was cheaper to fly the entire cast
                 and crew over here from Hollywood than it
                 would have been to build anything so
                 dreadful from scratch.

JOE   We must replace despair with hope. Not Tony
                 Blair hope. Real hope. (*Beat*). So how do we
                 break the mould of British politics?

A moment's silence.

                 Nothing? (*Beat*). Anyone?

MAGGIE   What about Brexit?

Everyone laughs or groans.

                 Sorry.

SAM   "Brexit means Brexit"

69

They all laugh again, more loudly.

JOE I campaigned against Brexit/

ANNE But you couldn't persuade your constituents/

SAM 63 per cent leave was it?

JOE Maybe, but they still voted for me.

ANNE I'm sorry to break it to you, but that wasn't entirely because you're you.

JOE Even at the by-election?

LIZ At the by-election you no longer represented the status quo.

ANNE Brexit, the rise of Corbyn, your by-election victory – all part of the same phenomenon.

SAM And now it looks like President Pence will be getting his own mandate.

MAGGIE Christ on a bike. I thought Trump was the lowest we could get. We didn't know when we were well off.

SAM When Trump was elected, my little wee sister thought it was the best thing ever.

MAGGIE How old was she?

SAM Six or seven. She genuinely believed the Orangemen were taking over the world. I swear to God.

MAGGIE	Now they have Mike Pence and we have Brexit/
ANNE	After a fashion/
SAM	In truth, what always mattered was not how hard or soft it was/
MAGGIE	But what we do with it.
LIZ	Where have I heard that before?
SAM	Ewwww.
MAGGIE	Brexit has been a national humiliation.
JOE	We're rule takers, not rule makers.
SAM	I've been just taking for years too. Suits me fine and dandy.
LIZ	The entire country went arse over Brexit.
MAGGIE	What matters is why people voted for Brexit. For millions of them, it was nothing to do with Europe at all.
ANNE	European immigrants.
JOE	Steady!
ANNE	Not about race. About numbers. Culture.
MAGGIE	There certainly was a grim pleasure in it. You know, watching MPs with the referendum gun at their heads, sullenly voting through something most of them hated.

SAM	Like forcing children to eat liver.
MAGGIE	Except liver is actually good for you.
JOE	Maybe that's all the people wanted? To emasculate the political class.
MAGGIE	That's the risk of a referendum.
LIZ	A Parliament of Eunuchs.
SAM	The British attitude to Europe reminds me of my parents' cat. He scratches the door to leave, so you get up and open it. Then he just sits there licking his balls. This country's been licking its own balls for too long.
ANNE	It's obvious to me why people voted for Brexit/
SAM	It is?
ANNE	Of course. You can't understand because you're an insider.
SAM	An insider? I'm an insider? I only moved here nine... ten... months ago. You've been here since the Norman invasion.
ANNE	Just for once, stop sniping and pay attention. There are millions of people in this country/
SAM	You don't say/
ANNE	Millions of people who have been in retreat all their lives. Some are desperately poor Labour voters in the North and some are filthy rich

Tories in the south, but they have this in common. The pits have closed, the factories have gone, the High Streets are ghost towns – charity shops, pawnbrokers and vaping stores. Their kids do drugs, join gangs, carry knives or just lose themselves on the Internet/

JOE   Go on Anne/

ANNE   Oh I will. Since the last war, their way of life has been completely laid to waste – and once, just for once, they were able to come together and be on the winning side/

LIZ   In the referendum/

ANNE   In the referendum – and who can begrudge them that? For once they won – and they won't let that go. (*Beat*). Nor should they.

MAGGIE Even if it costs them their jobs?

ANNE   Jobs? Jobs? What jobs? Packing mail-order boxes? The referendum happened, but Labour and the Tories have honoured neither the spirit nor the letter of Brexit/

SAM   They wouldn't, would they?

ANNE   No. And people are angry. The way I see it is this. We live in a country where most people are patriotic and fear losing their culture and heritage. Most people also care about inequality, unfairness and social justice.

SAM	You can't say the same for their political leaders.
JOE	You certainly cannot.
ANNE	Yet most people on the Left argue that social justice belongs exclusively to them, while almost everyone on the Right believes they and only they – have a privileged freehold on patriotic sentiment and the Union Jack. So why the Hell/
JOE	So why the Hell can't a political party do both – promote radical social justice and greater equality, whilst also cherishing our traditions and defending our national pride and integrity?
ANNE	Precisely. And might that not be the unique alchemy of Joe Newman?
Beat	
JOE	Some colleagues are talking to me.
LIZ	Talking? About what?
JOE	Defection. Realignment.
SAM	Labour MPs?
JOE	MPs, yes. And not just Labour.
SAM	Not Tories? Ugh. How many?
ANNE	More than fifty.

SAM	[*TO ANNE*] How come you know about this?
ANNE	Work it out for yourself.
Beat	
SAM	What about an opinion poll? The pollsters could ask a totally unbiased question. You know, "Would you vote for a new party..."/
JOE	Not necessarily party/
SAM	OK, "political movement, force, whatever, if it was amazing and fantastic and full of lovely people who all want the best for the country?"
ANNE	And it could win.
MAGGIE	Yes, and if it could win.
LIZ	Would a polling company provide something that blatant for you? All the others laugh.
SAM	Oh yeah. No problem. Tell them the result you want and they'll ask the right questions.
JOE	Ninety thousand you said?
LIZ	Ninety thousand?
SAM	Quid. In donations.
LIZ	Chuffing Nora!
JOE	Let's spend some of it.

INTERLUDE

AV – A TV broadcast.

PRESENTER   Today a shock poll suggests Joe Newman could sweep all the way into Number 10 Downing Street. The poll, by Alright Guv, suggests Mr Newman could win over 40 per cent of the vote, potentially giving him a majority in the House of Commons.

JOE   I am delighted, but not surprised. The country is going to the dogs. And no one else at Westminster seems to give a damn.

INTERVIEWER But is this poll reliable? Your critics claim the questions were heavily slanted in your favour.

JOE   Typical. More sour grapes. The people who conducted this poll are professional men and women, people of integrity. It's grossly unfair to traduce them in that way.

PRESENTER   Well, you heard it here first. The squall of Teesside could yet develop into a major storm right across Britain.

Back in the office, LIZ is no longer present – and JOE, MAGGIE, ANNE & SAM have shifted around.

JOE   So, a new force promoting robust, common-sense policies/

SAM   Could win over a third of the vote.

JOE   Which could deliver what? A few dozen seats?

SAM	It could be a lot more than that.
ANNE	Are you sure?
SAM	A win is a win. Blair won outright with 35 per cent. Cameron with 37.
JOE	Look what happened to them.
ANNE	I wouldn't mind their bank balances.
MAGGIE	Nor would I.
ANNE	There's the 48 per cent and there's the 52 per cent. It's two nations out there now, not one.
JOE	I still believe in One Nation. I want to bring people back together.
SAM	Send for Gareth Southgate!
ANNE	Call me Devil's Advocate if you will, but how can you ever hope to have "One Nation" – without a shared language - and shared basic values?
SAM	Really, we need to hit the G spot of Brexiteers. The "B spot".
MAGGIE	We can start with public services.
JOE	Specifically?
MAGGIE	The fire service. Teachers. Nurses. Police. Paramedics. Lousy pay, long hours, low morale.

JOE	Anything else? I don't want ideology here. Real-life examples, please; and practical, real-world solutions.
ANNE	OK. Transport. It's always coming up. Bus lanes, potholes, the lousy train service to London.
SAM	We should re-nationalise the railways. End contracting out.
MAGGIE	Inequality?
SAM	Yes, but inequality of what?
MAGGIE	Life opportunities. Income. Educational standards. Everything, basically. It's a very unequal society. Wickedly so.
ANNE	YouTube air heads, Instagram so-called celebrities and top footballers earning millions, while everyone else struggles to make ends meet.
SAM	Freedom of speech. The right to offend. Remember that student who got hounded out of that Sixth Form College, just for saying he thought girls were rubbish at football. Yeah. Schools.
JOE	Schools? Good thing?
MAGGIE	Yes, good thing. Very good thing. My daughter's a teacher and she's always threatening to quit.

ANNE	Why?
MAGGIE	The pressure.
ANNE	From what?
MAGGIE	Well, the kids used to have support at home/
ANNE	And?
MAGGIE	And now a lot of them don't. And/
ANNE	And?
MAGGIE	Half the class – well, nearly half/
ANNE	Yes?
MAGGIE	They don't have English.
ANNE	At all?
MAGGIE	Not at home.
ANNE	And?
MAGGIE	And the teachers have to give them special coaching. In theory there should be support, but/
ANNE	But/
MAGGIE	There are no resources for it.
ANNE	So we expect teachers to pick up the pieces of a broken society, but then we treat them as chancers not professionals.

MAGGIE	We persecute kids with tests, when we should be teaching them to become good citizens, not just exam fodder.
JOE	I take your point.
SAM	And we need cleaner hospitals.
ANNE	Bring back matrons.
SAM	Carry On Matron.
ANNE	I'm sick and tired of the Scots whingeing and whining about Westminster. Let them go. Then we can sit back and laugh as their economy goes tits up.
MAGGIE	When I'm in the village I have to drive 10 miles to get cash. We should stop the banks closing their rural branches and cash machines.
ANNE	Knife crime. Twice this year gangs have spilt blood on my street. In broad daylight.
MAGGIE	What's the solution to that?
SAM	Make an example of some of those vicious bastards?
ANNE	No. We should instil some discipline into the younger generation. A sense of service.
JOE	National service?

ANNE   Why not? Give them a sense of responsibility. Duty to nation. Active citizenship. Patriotism.

Tiny beat.

SAM   Fairness? "It's so unfair".

ANNE   Constituents say it all the time.

MAGGIE   Remember what George Orwell said – Britain is like a family, but with the wrong members in charge.

SAM   We're not much like a family now. (*Beat*). Maybe an abusive one.

ANNE   And the wrong people are still in charge.

JOE   So what is it? What has made this society so fractured and angry?

SAM   That's easy.

ANNE   Easy? So go on then, Oh Great Oracle, I'm all ears…

SAM   There's no real political debate any more. We just accept what the corporations want, what the parties say, what economics seem to dictate, And it works very nicely for the few, but not the many.

ANNE   It makes a small number of very privileged people very, very rich/

MAGGIE   But for the majority it means living
                constantly on the breadline. A life of
                insecurity, zero-hours contracts and no
                employment rights/

JOE   This does sound a bit like Jeremy Corbyn all
                over again – and look what happened to him.

SAM   People are still crying out for the radicalism.
                They just want to hear it from someone
                credible. Someone without all the dodgy
                baggage.

MAGGIE   So what's the missing ingredient?

ANNE   Leadership?

SAM   Genuine empathy with how people are
                feeling? What they've lost?

MAGGIE   The destruction of communities. Young
                people priced out of their own towns and
                cities.

ANNE   And what caused the housing crisis?
                Uncontrolled immigration.

SAM   That's basically true. Simple supply and
                demand.

ANNE   The numbers game.

Beat. There is palpable tension and awkwardness in the room.

                Mass migration has been deliberately,
                knowingly used to drive down wages,
                undercutting the wages of the working poor.

SAM   Pay poverty wages to immigrants, to do the
               jobs home-grown Brits refuse to do.

ANNE   The Tories promised to put an end to it – only
               "highly skilled" migrants allowed, ha ha – but
               everyone knew that was impossible. Every
               care home in the land would have closed down
               in a year.

MAGGIE   It's exploitation, pure and simple. Minimum
               wage if you're lucky. Bar work, care homes,
               scrubbing hospital wards for crap pay.

SAM   Why can't we sort our own shit out?
               Literally.

ANNE   Every day we import cheap labour. And
               every day our society becomes more stressed
               and fragmented.

SAM   The right turn a blind eye to it because their
               chums in business make a fat profit out of it/

ANNE   And the left encourage it, because it creates a
               political base for them.

JOE   So this is the elephant in the room?

SAM   Elephant? Indian or African?

ANNE   Does it matter?

MAGGIE   It matters to the elephant.

ANNE   The point about the elephant is, it doesn't
               belong here.

| MAGGIE | Immigration, though, Joe? |

| SAM | It's at the heart of why so many people are anxious and angry. |

| JOE | I know. I know. |

They all appear drained. MAGGIE slips away.

AV INTERLUDE

| PRESENTER | Rumours at Westminster suggest as many as 60 MPs, from across the parties, may join a new party led by Joe Newman. Pressure grows on Mr Newman to make a clear statement about his intentions. I now speak to the eminent political scientist, Professor Sir John Curtice, about what the prospects might be for a new party led by Mr Newman. |

PROFESSOR SIR JOHN CURTICE

Back in the office, sometime has evidently elapsed. Now just JOE, ANNE & SAM. A number of populist policies have been scrawled across the walls, with some poll data: "Have politicians been honest about immigration? Yes – 7%. No – 84%". "Has immigration damaged social cohesion? Yes – 74%. No – 11%." "Is immigration still too high? No – 17%. Yes 75%." "Would you consider voting for a new political force, based upon traditional British values of fairness, freedom and national identity? Definitely – 24%. Possibly – 47%".

| ANNE | The fact you came to this country as a child gives you a perfect "get out of jail free" card. |

| SAM | No one can accuse you of hating immigrants. |

84

JOE   Wouldn't people find this stuff a bit weird,
               coming from me? I'm a former Labour MP,
               not Katie fucking Hopkins.

ANNE   Nixon can go to China.

SAM   What?

ANNE   Because Nixon was so right wing, no one
               could ever accuse him of being a Commie
               sympathiser. So he could go to Peking
               without anyone suspecting him of selling out.
               It's an old Chinese saying.

SAM   If it's about Nixon it can't be that old. Mind
               you, if you know about it, then it probably
               dates back to the mid-Confucius era?

JOE   You know, I'm not sure I've ever seen an
               immigrant in Finborough.

SAM   A couple of taxi drivers maybe – and that
               Polish deli on the High Street. Actually I
               don't think they're even from Poland. They
               sound kind of Geordie/

ANNE   Even worse. Listen, a tough line on
               immigration could make perfect sense to
               Labour voters in the North, Tory voters in
               the South – and floating voters everywhere.

JOE   Won't Tory voters be put off by the rest of
               these policies?

SAM	Not necessarily. They aren't all stockbrokers you know. Most of them also suffer from shite trains, closed banks and dirty hospitals.
ANNE	Why do we give citizenship to every child born here? Illegal migrant has child. Child has citizenship. Whole family stays. Other European countries don't do that.
JOE	Fair point, I suppose.
ANNE	Full passport checks coming in and going out. About time we had those.
SAM	Green cards?
ANNE	We could impose a trial period for living here.
SAM	Like a provisional driving licence.
ANNE	Only for longer. Ten years maybe? If you seriously do want to control your borders – and we all know the voters overwhelmingly do – then you must be willing to do things that can be portrayed as callous or cruel. Turn people away. Forcibly deport people.
JOE	Who are you Anne? This is all so (*tiny beat*) unexpected. I feel like I never knew anything about you.
ANNE	Well, you never asked, did you?
JOE	I'm sorry.
ANNE	I'll tell you who I am. I'm the one who takes all the calls from your angry constituents.

	The one who does her best to make things better for them. I'm the one who listens to them. And now I speak for them.
SAM	And to win over Essex man…
ANNE	Or Doncaster man.

Beat

JOE	Or Finborough man…
ANNE	…and woman…
SAM	…you must first declare war on Islington Man.
JOE	You know, I think I preferred it when you hated each other.
ANNE	We still do.
SAM	Purely a temporary marriage of convenience.
JOE	We've made good progress. I have to go. I'm already late for that meeting about the new school/
SAM	I've drafted something for you.
JOE	Thank you. Very helpful.

JOE exits.

SAM	That was very impressive.
ANNE	I believe everything I said.
SAM	If it carries Joe into Number 10/

ANNE   Then you'll believe in it too.

SAM   We understand one another I think.

ANNE   Oh yes. No problems there.

ANNE exits, with a spring in her step.

INTERVAL

During the interval, a copy of Sam's note to Joe could be handed out to members of the audience.

SCENE 15

AV

PRESENTER Just a week after Joe Newman's high-profile speech on the dangers of large-scale immigration, a new poll today suggests that over a third of voters would like to see him as Prime Minister. He and his staff are understood to be building up a rudimentary party organisation and signing up potential party members in their thousands.

SCENE 16

THE WESTMINSTER OFFICE.

SAM   So, is she married?

JOE   I don't think so. I honestly have no idea.

SAM   You're joking?

JOE   Not at all. She's worked for me for almost five years and she's more of a mystery to me than ever. Until the last few weeks, I never even discussed politics with her.

SAM   That's certainly changed.

JOE   She's never mentioned a partner.

SAM   Maybe she's a big old lesbian, out on the pull every night.

JOE   Fuckaduck, there's a thought.

SAM   She has this gigantic dildo/

ANNE enters.

ANNE   Good morning.

SAM   Good moaning.

SAM has the giggles.

ANNE   Your guest has arrived. I'll go and fetch him.

ANNE exits.

JOE	[*TO SAM*] So remind me. Who exactly is this person?
SAM	He's the doyen of political campaigning.
JOE	Doyen? He looks about 14.
SAM	Well, that's what his website says. "Doyen". And he's older than that.
JOE	Like 15?
SAM	[*Reading*] He's a "great survivor in an industry with a notoriously high attrition rate".
JOE	Presumably not the consequence of over work. Well, I've never heard of him.
SAM	Exactly. That's part of the skill.
JOE	Has he offered you a job?
SAM	No.
JOE	You shagging him?
SAM	No!
JOE	He shagging you then?
SAM	No. Ewwww.
JOE	I should never have agreed to see him. Bloody con men, the lot of them. PR people are all tactics and no strategy.
SAM	What the Hell does that mean?

JOE	I haven't a clue. I'm already talking like him. It must be contagious.
SAM	Please, just hear him out. He's not charging us anything.
JOE	He's not worth anything. Bloody PR men. Such phoneys. So two-faced.

ANNE ushers in the PR MAN.

	Hi! Great to see you. Thank you so much for finding the time/
PR MAN	I'm here to give you advice because I can see you need advice.
JOE	OK. And what, exactly, is your advice?
PR MAN	Public relations is a delicate amalgam of art and science.
JOE	[*GIGGLING*] Oh it is, is it?
PR MAN	Some compare our greatest practitioners with the legendary, metaphysical alchemists of yore.
JOE	Of my what?
PR MAN	Yore. Yore. Ancient times. I have a possible slogan for you.
JOE	Oh yes?
PR MAN	Vote for a New Man in No.10.
JOE	Oh.

PR MAN	It's a pun you see.
JOE	Yes. I got that. I can't believe we didn't think of it ourselves.
SAM	Of course, it wouldn't have worked in the by-election, because you were a Newman, but not/
JOE	A new man. Well spotted, Sam.
SAM	More of an old man/
JOE	Yes, thank you. Top of the class.
PR MAN	My next piece of vital advice. Don't be too posh.
JOE	Sorry. Too posh?
PR MAN	Too posh. If you're too posh, you'll scare off Labour voters.
JOE	I'm not posh.
PR MAN	Or too regional.
JOE	"Regional"? Let me guess/
PR MAN	And don't be too gay.
JOE	What the Hell does that mean? Don't wear lippie and a tutu on live TV?
PR MAN	Don't act gay.
JOE	"Act gay"?
PR MAN	Straight acting.

JOE   You mean pretend? Act straight? You've lost me.

SAM   No. "Straight acting". It's a term of art/

PR MAN   Straight acting/

SAM   And it requires more than a dishevelled suit, a beer gut and hiding away your Kylie CDs.

JOE   Dishevelled? Beer gut? Kylie?!?

PR MAN   Straight acting.

JOE   Yes, you said that. Can't I just be myself?

PR MAN   Never been tried. Sounds insane.

JOE   I'm just an ordinary bloke.

PR MAN   Exactemundo. That's precisely your strength. Most politicians are so bloody weird. Freaks. Your very ordinariness. It's unique. Compelling. We just need to polish that ordinariness a bit.

JOE   Meaning?

PR MAN   It might help if you pretend to like football.

JOE   You haven't done much homework, have you? I do like football.

PR MAN   Great. That's great. Even better.

SAM smiles and nods, encouragingly. ANNE shakes her head.

JOE	I even know the difference between West Ham and Aston Villa. I've supported Boro since I was a boy. I have a season ticket.
PR MAN	Great. Which borough?
JOE	Jesus. Boro. Middlesbrough.
PR MAN	That's a team?
JOE	Yes. (*Beat*). And a place.
PR MAN	If you say so.
JOE	I was on their books as a kid.
PR MAN	Books? Books are good. Just don't seem too intellectual.
JOE	Right...
PR MAN	Great. That's great. Fabulous.
ANNE	Fabulous?
PR MAN	Fabulous.
JOE	Fabulous?
PR MAN	Fabulous. Really fabulous. Saves me a lot of work. Now, Joshua Phillips/
JOE	Excuse me?
PR MAN	I assume he'll be supporting you?
JOE	Supporting me? He hates me.

PR MAN	It would be perfect for him to be out there as your "plus one". Your "special friend".
JOE	Josh isn't/
PR MAN	"Josh". Nice.
JOE	Phillips isn't one of my supporters. He's not my friend. If anything, he's my enemy.
PR MAN	Enemy? There's a lot of negativity in that word.
JOE	Really? You think so?
PR MAN	I would say he's your (*tiny beat*) inspiration. He inspired you on this journey of yours.
JOE	He really didn't, you know.
PR MAN	He's also very telegenic.
ANNE	Certainly an improvement on someone I could mention [*looks at SAM*].
JOE	He was part of my private life, not my public life. A tiny part. (*SAM sniggers or raises his eyebrows*). A tiny part of my life. Fuck off, Sam. So, no, he won't be involved.

The PR MAN looks surprised and faintly nauseous. SAM looks increasingly mortified. ANNE gloats.

PR MAN	Maybe Samuel here could talk to him for you, persuade him to help? Not for anything ostentatious. (*Beat*). No hugging or kissing.

JOE	This is weird.
PR MAN	Just act normal. Try to act normal.
JOE	Act normal?
SAM	Samuel?!?
JOE	Normal?
PR MAN	Normal.
JOE	Will you stop repeating everything I say back at me? Is that all you PR people do?
ANNE	Evidently.
PR MAN	I am sensing an attitude which may not be entirely constructive/
JOE	I'm sorry, but I think this is a total waste of time, for all of us.
ANNE	Congratulations, Sam. Another triumph.

SCENE 17

A V

OBSERVER   Well yes, I suppose what I am saying is that Joe Newman is a "nice guy". An ordinary Joe, as they say in the United States. And it's certainly true that, for someone who is making waves, he has remarkably few enemies. Do I like him? I certainly don't agree with everything he's been saying, but yes, yes I do like him. Why not?

SCENE 18

MAGGIE'S OFFICE.

JOE   Can I truly represent my constituents, without taking full account of their views?

MAGGIE   By which you mean their prejudices?

JOE   One person's prejudices can be another's opinions.

MAGGIE   The British are a tolerant people/

JOE   Yes, of course they are, but that tolerance has been stretched to breaking point. Mass immigration is unfair. And the one thing we won't tolerate/

MAGGIE   We?

JOE   Yes, we. The one thing we won't tolerate is unfairness. (*Beat*). You seem upset with me.

MAGGIE   Upset? "I'm not upset, just a little disappointed". I sound like something out of a 1940s melodrama.

JOE   What's wrong?

MAGGIE   Perhaps I just thought you had better taste, sounder judgement and a kinder heart. It's all so easy.

JOE   I'm not going to hurt anyone.

MAGGIE	Oh aren't you? Tell me, do you think it's healthy and right to say these things? Do you believe everything you're saying?
JOE	It all makes perfect sense to me.
MAGGIE	That's not what I asked.
JOE	Look, Maggie.
MAGGIE	Never mind "Look, Maggie". Do you believe in it all? In your heart, your mind, your guts? With passion? Will you fight for it, go to your grave for it?
JOE	Maggie, we've known each other a long time and/
MAGGIE	Do you believe in it?
JOE	Yes, yes I think I do.
MAGGIE	You think you do?
JOE	I do. It's that simple. Alright? Absolutely 100 per cent. (*Beat*). You know, in the beginning, the only person who came to all my meetings was a campaigner against badger culls.
MAGGIE	And what's your policy on that?
JOE	Do you know, I haven't a clue. Not sure I've ever met a badger. Well, Alistair Darling or Norman Lamont I suppose. A policy on badgers I really can make up as I go along.

MAGGIE   And that distinguishes it in some way from all your other policies?

JOE   Kill the bloody badgers. That's a policy. They don't vote, so let 'em have it, the little bastards!

They laugh.

MAGGIE   Just remember: "For every complex problem there is an answer that is clear, simple, and wrong".

JOE   That's very good. Yours?

MAGGIE   No. Mencken's.

JOE   Alan Menken?

MAGGIE   H.L. Mencken. Philosopher and wit. Who's Alan Menken?

JOE   A composer.

MAGGIE   Contemporary of Mozart?

JOE   Disney films. Stage musicals.

MAGGIE   Seriously?

JOE   There's nothing wrong with Disney. The Little Mermaid. Beauty and the Beast. Frozen.

MAGGIE   You camp old thing.

JOE	Oh let it go. Anyway, you're hardly the arbiter of high culture. You watch "Bake Off".
MAGGIE	"Bake Off"? I hate it.
JOE	Oh yes, but you always watch it.
MAGGIE	Don't you?
JOE	No. I've never seen it. (*Beat*). Is my shameful secret safe with you?
MAGGIE	I've always believed you have greatness in you Joe. Now get out there, get yourself elected and prove it.

SCENE 19

AV INSERT (*V. Short, to cover scene change*)

JOE   My favourite television show? Why, this one
                 of course. [*Laughter and a little applause from
                 the studio audience*]. Well, I do enjoy the soaps
                 and I am a big, big fan of Bake Off...

SCENE 20

A BAR OR CLUB

SAM and JOSH on a dance floor. A chance encounter.

JOSH	Well, well. Joe Newman's rent boy.
SAM	Thought you'd be out wrecking the Labour Party. Sorry, on the campaign.
JOSH	Well you'd know all about being a camp pain. Haven't seen you since that night at Joe's flat.
SAM	He didn't want you there.
JOSH	Oh. He seemed happy to give me his time. About three minutes with him usually suffices, if memory serves.
SAM	So you're shite in bed.
JOSH	At least I've been there.
SAM	Don't we know it. Proves Joe isn't a size queen.
JOSH	You've never had him, have you?
SAM	I work for him.
JOSH	You want him though, don't you? I can see it in your eyes.
SAM	Oh, fuck you. You're just a maggot feeding on Labour's corpse.

JOSH   Our movement is the best hope this country has had in generations. Of bringing justice and opportunity into the lives of the many, not the few.

SAM   I'm sorry, but I grew out of pathetic Marxist fantasies before my voice broke.

JOSH   So recently?

SAM   We'll destroy you.

JOSH   Sweetheart, I don't believe that for one moment. But even if you did, all you'd do next is steal most of our policies.

JOSH holds SAM, firmly but not without tenderness, then kisses him. They stare at each other for a moment.

SCENE 21

A V

OBSERVER King John signed Magna Carta in the year 1215 at Runnymede, King John signed Magna Carta in the year 1215 at Runnymede, paving the way for freedom and democracy. Joe Newman chose that very same spot at 12.15 today, to launch the first new, national, parliamentary force for forty years – the so-called Popular People's Movement. A letter of support from over 100 prominent business leaders appeared in today's edition of the Times newspaper – and 32 Members of Parliament attended the launch event, making the new PPM already the third largest grouping in the House of Commons. It claims to have over 100,000 paid-up supporters already – and intends to start contesting elections immediately.

SCENE 22

Joe, sitting, alone

MAGGIE   Don't make promises you can't keep/

JOE   I'm trying not to/

MAGGIE   Just get elected.

JOE   "Just" get elected?

MAGGIE   Once you're elected, then you can do all the
                  good things/

JOE   The good things?

MAGGIE   The good things I know you want to do/

JOE   You know what I want to do?

MAGGIE   Of course.

JOE   I'm not sure I do.

MAGGIE   Promise not to act in anger.

JOE   [*ANGRY*] I'm not angry. (*Tiny beat*). Oh.

MAGGIE   Do what's right.

JOE   Of course.

MAGGIE   Right for the country, but also for you.

JOE   That's easy to say/

MAGGIE   Err on the side of kindness.

JOE   Don't I always?

MAGGIE	Retain your humanity. Otherwise you won't be you any longer.
JOE	Believe me, I am trying.
LIZ	You're certainly trying.
SAM	Do whatever it takes.
JOE	Really?
ANNE	Say whatever you have to say.
JOE	Anything?
LIZ	Joe, don't listen to them.
ANNE	We can win. Win big.
LIZ	Joe, I'm worried about you/
JOE	Don't fuss.
ANNE / SAM	Power!
LIZ	Someone has to.
ANNE	We'll take care of him.
SAM	He's fine.
JOE	I'm fine.
LIZ	Are you?
JOE	I'm enjoying myself/
LIZ	I don't like what you're saying about immigrants, you know/

JOE	About immigration.
LIZ	Same difference.
JOE	No more Mr. Nice Guy.
LIZ	But you are a nice guy. Stay nice.
JOE	Nice guys don't win in politics/
LIZ	Why not?
JOE	They just don't.
LIZ	It doesn't have to be like that.
JOE	I'm no one else's mouthpiece.
LIZ	I don't know if that makes things better or worse.
JOSH	You talk horse-shite.
JOE	Excuse me?
JOSH	Horse-shite. Fascistic horse-shite. Total horse-shite.
JOE	It's your responsibility.
JOSH	Come again?
JOE	You started this.
JOSH	You're a snake-oil salesman. A fraud. A total wankhobbit.
JOE	A wankhobbit? What the fuck is a wankhobbit?

JOSH points at JOE, as if to say "You are!"

JOSH   I can't believe I loved you once.

JOE   I loved you.

JOSH   You used me.

JOE   You tried to destroy me.

JOSH   I love you. We/

JOE   We?

JOSH   It doesn't matter.

JOE   It matters.

ANNE   You can give the people their country back. Tell it like it is. Honesty. Patriotism. Moral courage. Tell people who's to blame.

JOE   To blame?

ANNE   For the mess we're in.

JOSH   Bankers.

MAGGIE   Wall Street.

ANNE   Immigrants.

SAM   Muslims.

ALL FOUR   Bankers. Wall Street.

ANNE / SAM   Muslims.

ANNE   Immigrants.

SAM	Immigrants.
LIZ	Immigrants, Joe? Immigrants?
MAGGIE	Liz, you don't understand.
ANNE	She never does.
JOSH	She loves you.
SAM	She's part of the problem.
ANNE	She and people like her.
SAM	Urban liberals.
ANNE	Guardian readers.
JOSH	Selfie takers.
LIZ	People who walk on cracks in the pavement.
MAGGIE	Drivers who text.
SAM	Ambulance chasers.
JOSH	Coughs and sneezes spread diseases.
ANNE	The leeches draining our society.
JOE	Leeches?
ANNE	Of course. And you know the solution.
JOE	I do?
ANNE	Strong government.
MAGGIE	A thumping majority.

SAM	Loyal advisers, who think outside the box.
JOE	Box?
JOSH	Paint Buckingham Palace with a rainbow.
LIZ	Move Stonehenge three feet to the left.
ANNE	Bring back national service.
SAM	Restore national pride.
JOSH	Slaughter the first born.
LIZ	Begin the beguine.
ANNE	Control our borders.
SAM	Reaffirm our native culture.
ANNE	Make Britain British again.
MAGGIE	Which side are you on Joe? Which side are you on?
JOE	The underdog. The side of the underdog.
JOSH	Woof, woof!
ANNE	The decent, working people/
LIZ	The white people, she means/
ANNE	The decent, working people.
SAM	The media love you Joe.
ANNE	Tory voters love you Joe.
MAGGIE	Labour voters love you Joe.

JOSH	Fascist voters love you Joe.
LIZ	I love you Joe.
JOSH	I love you Joe.
ALL FIVE	We all love you Joe.
	Joe!
	Joe!
	Joe!

JOE is alone again.

SCENE 23

AV INSERT

PRESENTER For the fourth week running, the new PPM
has maintained its commanding lead in the
opinion polls, with just over 50 per cent
support. It appears to be drawing its support
equally from Labour and the Conservatives.
Even some Liberal Democrat voters have
been switching to it.

SCENE 24

A STUDIO

JOE   [*TO SAM*] Suddenly I'm not sure it was such
                   a good idea to do this live. (*Beat*). Not that I
                   have much choice now. How long do we have?

SAM   You'll be fine. Your script will be running
                   right in front of you. Deep breaths...

*For a moment JOE looks around, seemingly disorientated. He rubs
his temples, then clasps his hands together, muttering softly to
himself. He breathes fast, shallowly. There is pain etched into his
face. The moment passes.*

                   Are you OK?

JOE   I don't know. I'm still not sure I'm doing the
                   right thing.

GOPHER   (*VOICE ONLY*) Going live in sixty. I'll count
                   you down from ten.

SAM   Well you'd better make your mind up pretty
                   sharpish/

JOE   I bumped into the chief whip this morning.
                   She says she never told the press. About me.

SAM   About you what?

JOE   About me and Josh/

GOPHER   Going into the twenty/

SAM   And you believed her?

115

JOE	I'm not sure. I always assumed she did it. And yet she did seem/
GOPHER	Fifteen/
JOE	But who else would want to do that to me? Stir up the press like that?
SAM	I don't know. I honestly have no/
GOPHER	And the ten, nine, eight, seven, six.
SAM	Joe, calm down. You're on.
JOE	Yes. Well, here goes nothing.

The final five seconds are counted down silently. JOE gathers himself. Steps outside himself.

A VOICE	(*AV*) There now follows a broadcast by the Popular People's Movement.
JOE	(*In the room*) Just three months ago, I resigned as a Member of Parliament. It was not an easy decision. Ever since I was a schoolboy I had dreamed of sitting where Disraeli, Gladstone and Churchill once sat. Where the fate of our nation has been decided across the centuries. The polls and the pundits predicted humiliation, but I had faith. And I never lost that faith – my faith in the decency and common sense of the people I served.

I knew them and they knew me. My faith was rewarded and I am, once again, the Member of Parliament for a beautiful constituency |

that represents the best of British. But what remains of Britain, of England? Our traditions have been mocked, scorned and discarded by the politically correct establishment. We should be proud to be British. And we have every right to be proud of being British. One nation, united by a common language and shared core values. The tolerance. The acceptance of difference. The gentle give and take of our political discourse. Religious moderation. The poetry of Shakespeare, Wordsworth and Eliot. Our countryside and open spaces.

Our fundamental freedoms, for which our forebears fought and died. Our right to speak our mind out. Our freedom to criticise, to mock, to ridicule, to laugh at others and to laugh at ourselves. To live the way we choose. Our bad teeth and our good manners. Peace and quiet. Ant and Dec. Rough and tumble. Cannon and Ball. Pomp and circumstance. Mel and Sue. Because, if we do value all of that, if we truly cherish it, then we must be prepared to fight for it. I pledge to fight to my dying breath, to defend our values, our borders, our historic freedoms and our way of life. We in the Popular People's Movement will make that stand. We will be free. This is my cause. This is our cause. Join me in it. Please. For all our sakes.

SAM Brilliant.

SCENE 25

REPORTER   We are hearing news of a mass defection of Members of Parliament to the PPM. (*Beat*). As I speak, Joe Newman is welcoming no fewer than 27 new MPs to his ranks - including two members of Labour's front bench – and calling for an immediate general election. If that is refused, it seems certain that 27 by-elections will follow, within a matter of weeks. The latest opinion polls suggest the PPM would be very well placed indeed to hold most, or even all, of these seats. The Government has lost all authority in the House of Commons. It is said to be on the brink of collapse.

118

SCENE 26

ANNE, SAM and LIZ

LIZ   I never wanted any of this. Some of the things
              he's saying/

ANNE   He's only telling the truth.

LIZ   It's not my truth.

ANNE   It's his truth now. You obviously didn't know
              him as well as you thought you did. You
              trained him brilliantly well.

LIZ   His supporters are a bunch of lager louts.

SAM   I'm not a lager lout.

LIZ   A lager top, maybe?

SAM   Actually, FYI, I'm more of a lager bottom.

LIZ   I had one of those once. Messy.

SAM   Why get your tits in such a tangle about it
              all?

LIZ   If you were a refugee adrift in the Med, the
              entire world would be telling you, no one
              wants you, you're nothing to us, you're no
              longer a human being, worthy of
              consideration.

ANNE   You're becoming hysterical.

LIZ   Don't those people deserve respect, the same
              respect we all receive?

119

SAM	You're being emotive. Emotional. Both.
LIZ	Yes, yes I am. Of course I am. Some refugees are gay like Joe and you too, Sam, desperate to escape persecution, torture or a brutal death.
SAM	That was a low blow.
LIZ	And suddenly you don't like a low blow?
ANNE	We can't just keep building on every bit of green to accommodate all comers. It's the numbers game.
LIZ	It's not a numbers game. It's a blame game. This isn't the Joe Newman I know and love. That Joe, he's a good man, a kind and generous man.
ANNE	Enough is enough. It's a constant refrain on the doorstep. Enough is enough.
SAM	And it's no longer enough for politicians just to mouth those words – "enough is enough". People expect us to do something. To change something.
LIZ	Then people need to be educated.
ANNE	Educated?
LIZ	On the benefits of immigration.
ANNE	Brainwashed you mean?
LIZ	I am honestly appalled/

ANNE	Appalled that the descendants of the people who built this country, who fought and died for it… Appalled that they want it back?
LIZ	We're never going to agree. We're just going to make one another angry.
ANNE	I'm not angry.
LIZ	No, I don't suppose you are. But plenty of other people are and you're happy to exploit that.
ANNE	Goodbye, Liz. And thank you for all your help. We couldn't have done it without you.

SCENE 27

PRESENTER   Of the 27 Labour and Conservative MPs who resigned to contest by-elections for the PPM a month ago, all but 3 have held their seats. 41 more MPs defected to the PPM enmasse this morning. The Prime Minister has summoned a meeting of the Cabinet at 11am. We expect an official statement by lunchtime.

JOE   (*VT*) By-elections would be utterly pointless. It's time for the nation to decide. And I believe the nation will choose the new politics that only the PPM can deliver.

SCENE 28

JOE and LIZ

JOE	So, at the last meeting the sad little arse handed me a manifesto.
LIZ	What sort of manifesto?
JOE	It's totally fucking insane. If I endorsed a single policy from it, the entire world'd conclude I'd lost my mind.
LIZ	Votes for animals?
JOE	Pretty much.
LIZ	Well you could always confine it to votes for indigenous species only. Your supporters might like that.
JOE	I've always supported animal welfare, but/
LIZ	But?
JOE	But my priority is people. If the human race dies out, Mozart and Shakespeare die with us.
LIZ	That would go down well on the council estates of Finborough.

LIZ produces a distinctive envelope.

JOE	Oh God. What is it now?
LIZ	Don't be like that. Some food for thought, from a writer you admire.

JOE	Why can't you just leave the serious politics to me?
LIZ	I shouldn't worry my little head about it? Too complex for little old me/
JOE	I'm not saying that.
LIZ	What are you saying, then, Joe?
JOE	All you do is carp and complain and try to undermine me. Don't you want me to succeed?
LIZ	Personally, yes. Politically, I'm not sure.
JOE	Well that's tough, because they're precisely the same thing.
LIZ	Bashing minorities, trashing your old party, setting up your new Hitler Youth/
JOE	Hitler Youth? Oh, Liz, get a grip, for fuck's sake.
LIZ	Me? Me, get a grip?
JOE	Politicians are either one thing or the other.
LIZ	You mean either decent, or else opportunistic shits/
JOE	Winners. Or losers. Thatcher or Kinnock. Blair or Hague. Miliband or Cameron/
LIZ	Cameron made us all losers. And look at him now. He daren't show his face in public. Do

	you want to end up the same way? Think about the immortal part of yourself.
JOE	My soul?
LIZ	No. You're a politician. You don't have one. Your reputation, Joe, your reputation.
JOE	I haven't been through all this/
LIZ	All what?
JOE	Deselection, the by-election, setting up the PPM/
LIZ	Yeah, all what? It's hardly been Robben fecking Island has it? A good shag, a few dodgy headlines and then nationwide adulation/
JOE	I haven't gone through all that, just to end up as a footnote. A might-have-been. A loser.
LIZ	Better that than a bloody fascist.
JOE	Liz, you don't know what you're/
LIZ	Talking about?
JOE	Saying. You don't know what you're saying.
LIZ	I know exactly what I'm saying. You're betraying everything you ever believed in. You're betraying me, you're betraying your own roots/

JOE   Liz, if I have to choose between listening to you/

LIZ   To me/

JOE   I'm going through with this. I'm sorry if that upsets you/

LIZ   If you think this is winning, I pity you.

JOE   If you think giving up now would be winning, then I pity you. No wonder you never made it in the theatre/

LIZ   Oh fuck you, Joe.

JOE   You're either with me or against me now.

LIZ   Draw your own conclusions.

LIZ exits. JOE ponders the envelope.

SCENE 29

AV REPORT

PRESENTER   The Government has technically been in a minority in the House of Commons for some time, but now it appears to have lost control entirely. We go across, live to Westminster...

A POLITICIAN SPEAKS.

SCENE 30

THE WESTMINSTER OFFICE.

JOE	That bloody beaver man was there again, picketing the studios.
SAM	Beaver man? You mean badger man.
JOE	Badger, beaver, same difference.
ANNE	That explains a lot.
JOE	They have to go to the country now. None of us has the people, the money or the appetite to fight 41 by-elections on a single day. (*Beat*). Is the manifesto ready?
SAM	Ready to roll.
JOE	Once it's published, everyone must stick to it.
SAM	Or else?
JOE	You bet. Or else.

JOE exits.

SAM	A wonderful thing, democracy.
ANNE	We should try it out some time.

SCENE 31

A Television News Report.

JOSH is on stage, watching the screen and reacting.

PRESENTER   The House of Commons has voted by an overwhelming majority for an immediate general election. The Prime Minister is now making the short journey from Downing Street to Buckingham Palace, to request a dissolution.

Joe Newman is the bookies' odds-on favourite to be the next Prime Minister.

JOE   Let me tell you about my father.

He didn't come to this country illegally.

He didn't come here with a begging bowl.

And he didn't come here because he wanted to transform it into an imitation of where he came from.

He adored this country.

INTERVIEWER And your point is?

JOE   He was a patriot. A proud, British patriot. And he brought me up to be a proud British patriot too. If every immigrant behaved like my dad chose to behave, think how strong this nation could be.

INTERVIEWER Don't we already have citizenship tests?

JOE   This isn't about ticking boxes. It's about culture and values. If you love us for what we are – if you want to embrace our values and our way of life – then you're welcome here. Otherwise, kindly go elsewhere. It's a simple enough proposition.

SCENE 32

AV – GE D 20

PPM 41, Lab 24, Con 22, Lib 7

SAM is on-stage, watching the screen.

PRESENTER   *(AV)* As we come to the end of the first full week of the campaign, two more PPM candidates have been suspended, making a total of seven so far, all of whom will still appear on local ballot papers. The PPM has fallen five points in the latest poll, to 41 per cent of the vote.

The V/T cuts to a shot of JOE on a street. He is surrounded by party activists with banners. A number of protesters are visible too, including a man with a large banner proclaiming "Save the Badgers. Cull Politicians, Not Innocent Animals'.

INTERVIEWER *(AV)* One of the suspended candidates said gay people should be barred from public office/

JOE   *(AV)* She has been suspended. I have no further comment to make.

INTERVIEWER *(AV)* Another denies the Holocaust ever happened/

JOE   *(AV)* I've said all I'm going to say. I'm here to discuss policies, not personalities.

INTERVIEWER (*AV*) Alright then. What about your proposal to reintroduce Section 28, which caused such misery to the LGBT community in the 1980s?

JOE draws up suddenly.

JOE   (*AV*) I'm sorry?

INTERVIEWER (*AV*) It's your stated policy, and I quote, to "put an end to public authorities targeting spending on minority groups, defined by any specified characteristic"/

JOE   (*AV*) That's not Section 28/

INTERVIEWER (*AV*) It amounts to the same thing, though, doesn't it?

JOE   (*AV*) That's not the intention. We want to stop taxpayers' money being squandered on buying votes/

INTERVIEWER (*AV*) But it'll have the same effect as Section 28, won't it? Surely LGBT people are 'defined by any specified characteristic'/

JOE   (*AV*) That's not the intention.

INTERVIEWER (*AV*) Haven't you been a little bit naive? An openly gay man – now, if not six months ago – attacking his own community, just for votes?

JOE   (*AV*) Listen, some smart-aleck little scrote at Labour HQ may have fed you this whippet shit, but I'm telling you, it's nonsense.

INTERVIEWER *(A V)* I'm reading your party's policy, not a briefing from anyone else/

JOE *(A V)* I've said all I have to say.

On-stage, SAM looks nauseous. JOE enters, at speed.

OK. Who the fuck put that stupid fucking policy into the manifesto? Section fucking 28. Just what this country needs.

SAM It isn't Section 28.

JOE I don't want the fucking line, I want the truth.

SAM Well, you signed it off. You signed off the manifesto.

JOE In the middle of a hectic day, whilst juggling fifteen other things, as you well know. It's your job to avoid this kind of fuck-up.

SAM There's a lot of support for this in the country.

JOE I don't care. You can shove this policy right up your no doubt well-lubricated/

SAM I've got the message.

JOE This would never have happened if Josh/

Beat

SAM If little Joshy had been here, doing my job?

JOE Bin it. Bin the policy. Now. (*He exits*)

SCENE 33

GE D-16

PPM 33, Lab 31, Con 23, Lib 7

OBSERVER   A snap-shot poll shows support for the PPM has fallen to below 40 per cent, for the first time ever. Can Joe Newman still aspire to become the most successful import from the Czech Republic since Budvar?

SAM alone on stage, talking into his mobile phone.

SAM   Yes, yes, I know, but we've dropped it. We've dropped the entire policy. Yes, I know, it was badly drafted. That's why we... That's why we dropped it. It's gone. No, of course we wouldn't resurrect it if we were in office. Look, I'm sorry, I've said all I'm going to say on this. I've got a call I need to take. Of course, we can speak later. (*Beat*). Hello? Yes, hello. Are you alright? You sound (*Beat*). Oh fuck. Is she OK? (*Beat*). OK, yes, I'll pass the message on as soon as I can. Of course I will.

SCENE 34

AV INSERT – GE D-14

PPM 31, Lab 31, Con 28, Lib 6

INTERVIEWER Your opponents say you are just UKIP Mark 2, a one-trick pony completely obsessed with immigration.

JOE Why is immigration the only thing you ever want to ask me about?

INTERVIEWER Well, perhaps because/

JOE It's becoming an obsession. The PPM is putting forward a comprehensive platform for government/

INTERVIEWER But your own media team/

JOE We will take the railways back into public ownership. We will increase the minimum wage by/

INTERVIEWER Your own media team/

JOE I know it won't affect you, but increasing the minimum wage by £3 an hour will change the lives of/

INTERVIEWER It's your own media team who keep telling us it's your policy on immigration that makes you different, that makes you unique.

JOE We will force the banks to operate in the public interest. We will/

INTERVIEWER Will? Or would?

JOE We will. If elected.

INTERVIEWER Joe Newman, thank you very much.

SCENE 35

GE D-13

A hospital room. MAGGIE enters, using a Zimmer frame. A couple of steps behind her is LIZ.

MAGGIE	As you can see, I've been butter.
LIZ	Oh, sweetheart.
MAGGIE	A "mini stroke", they call it. Felt like a bloody big one when it hit me.
LIZ	Will you recover?
MAGGIE	Mayhap. Mayhap? I rather like mayhap.
LIZ	So do I.
MAGGIE	But for now I'm knockered. Knackered. I fear I've hung up my campaigning roots for good.
LIZ	Boots.
MAGGIE	Yes. Birds. Words. [*Sighs*] What news of our great leader?
LIZ	Joe? Oh he's fine.

Beat

MAGGIE	I know he's using some tough lines, Liz, but he'd be a poor player otherwise.
LIZ	So a good man may say bad things?

137

MAGGIE	Ugly truths may serve the public better than beautiful pies. (*Beat*). Pies? Lies! Believe me. I survived the Blair years.
LIZ	Oh but his team. Anne's a total nutter. Sam's just a careerist. He's so shallow/
MAGGIE	You might say his shallowness runs deep. I've spent my life dealing with self-serving little toads/
LIZ	Turds?
MAGGIE	I did mean toads, but that too. Words, words. I keep/
LIZ	Forgetting them?
MAGGIE	Oh fuck off.

They both laugh.

LIZ	It all makes me wonder, who is the real Joe Newman?
MAGGIE	I suppose we shall find out spoon enough.

They have completed a circle of the room and exit together. As they do so, LIZ gently kisses MAGGIE's forehead.

SCENE 36

AV INSERT GE D-11

PPM 28, Lab 29, Con 30, Lib 9

PRESENTER   Joe Newman's opponents say he is beginning
to crack under the pressure of being what one
senior Labour figure termed a "one-man band
with no instruments to play". Mr Newman
himself claims PPM support has bounced
back since the controversy about a new
Section 28 and several PPM candidates being
disowned because of their extreme views. If
Mr Newman is beginning to crack, he was
showing little sign of it today, when he was
mobbed in the streets of Middlesbrough.

SCENE 37

GE D-10

JOE & SAM in a train carriage.

SAM   So what's this "private engagement" in London tomorrow at 4pm?

JOE   It's what it says. A private engagement. Don't worry your pretty little head about it.

SAM   It's him isn't it? Josh?

JOE   It's really none of your business/

SAM   What are you trying to achieve? You're not trying to make up with him?

JOE   He asked to talk to me and I'm going to talk to him. That's all.

SAM   I just think you have better things to do with your time.

JOE   Advice noted. Thank you.

SCENE 38

AV INSERT – GE D-9

PPM 28, Lab 30, Con 29, Lib 8

PRESENTER   Polls suggest support for Joe Newman and the PPM has bottomed out, but, with their predicted vote down from the mid-forties to the high twenties, they are now in serious danger of losing most of their 79 seats in Parliament.

JOE   Of course my opponents say I'm "talking the country down". That's what politicians always say, when they've run out of ideas and arguments and they know they've been rumbled.

SCENE 39

GE D-8

JOE & JOSH

JOE	Thank you for agreeing to see me. Eventually.
JOSH	Oh don't start. (*Tiny beat*). Anyway, how could I say no to an ex-future Prime Minister?
JOE	I guess you're entitled to that one. (*Beat*). I need your help.
JOSH	Oh. Now you need my help?
JOE	I need your support.
JOSH	What, a public endorsement?
JOE	More personal than that.
JOSH	Seriously?
JOE	Listen, I know you aren't comfortable with everything I've been saying/
JOSH	Not comfortable? Seriously? I used to think you were just a farty old "Centrist Dad". How wrong I was.
JOE	Go on, say it. I'm a fascist.
JOSH	Are you denying it?
JOE	It depends what you mean by "fascist" I suppose.

JOSH	Are you for real?
JOE	What's in a word?
JOSH	"I can't believe it's not fascism?"
JOE	Believe it. It's not fascism.

They both smile, awkwardly. The mood is changing.

JOSH	Go on, then. Persuade me.
JOE	I want the people of this country to pull together/
JOSH	All the people?
JOE	All the people, yes. To eradicate poverty, to reduce inequality/
JOSH	So the fatherland – or motherland – can unite around a strong leader/
JOE	If you like, yes/
JOSH	Just like Franco, or Mussolini, or Putin/
JOE	Or Stalin?
JOSH	Touche.
JOE	I'm certainly no racist.
JOSH	So you want to make white immigrants feel unwelcome too?
JOE	That's not what this is about/
JOSH	Racists are voting for you.

JOE	Racists vote for everybody. Well, maybe not the Lib Dems.
JOSH	No one votes for them.
JOE	True. Despite themselves they relax a little. I never mention race.
JOSH	It's what you think your supporters want to hear, though, isn't it?
JOE	No. Truthfully, no. This isn't about race/
JOSH	How long do you think this country would survive without immigrants? The biggest employers in Finborough are a family from India/
JOE	I know about all that/
JOSH	So what the Hell are you thinking? Is this just cynical opportunism?
JOE	It's about values and culture and pressure on public services and the green belt/
JOSH	Think of the pressure on public services when you deport the nurse, the cleaner, the porter. Who do you think will do those jobs? The sons and daughters of the landed aristocracy?
JOE	If the importance of those jobs were to be properly recognised, if they were to be paid according to their real value to society, instead of being ground down/

JOSH	Ha! Suddenly we're in serious danger of agreeing violently. (*Beat*). I think about you a lot.
JOE	I'm on television a lot.
JOSH	Sometimes I wonder if what you've been doing and saying has all been a way of getting back at me.
JOE	Ever the narcissist. No. This is bigger than you. Bigger than us.
JOSH	So you've never wanted to settle a score with me? The thought has never crossed your mind/
JOE	Settle a score? No.
JOSH	Really?
JOE	Really.
JOSH	Really, really?
JOE	Well, maybe a bit.
JOSH	Did you ever love me?
JOE	There's one way for you to find out. Come on board. Support what we're doing. I do truly intend to make this country fair and just and honest. We need you. I need you.
JOSH	Talk about a politician's answer.

JOE   If I win, I want you at my side. Please, think about it.

JOSH   I will think about it. But don't wait until after the election to prove you're a human being and a statesman. Show some decency. Some generosity of spirit. And do it now. Make that the foundation of your mandate.

JOE   Is that your price?

JOSH   It's my advice.

SCENE 40

AV – GE D-6

PPM 28, Lab 31, Con 30, Lib 7

CASHMAN   It's really difficult to know what to say to a man who seems to be living his life in a revolving door. What does spring to mind is a Biblical quote: "What should it profit a man or woman, if they gain the entire world, but sell their soul?" Having said that, I don't think Joe Newman has one to sell.

SCENE 41

Liz alone

She makes a call. Waits. Sighs.

LIZ   Joe. It's Liz. Look, I know how busy you are. I just wanted to let you know, the flat's fine. A lot of post, but that can wait until (*tiny beat*). Look, I know the polls aren't very good, but they so often are way wide of the mark. (*Beat*). OK, just in case, I'll make sure there's milk in your fridge the morning after the election. Only kidding. I can't wish you success, but I do wish you well. And I'm sending my love. I'm still here for you. [She hangs up]. I suppose I always shall be.

SCENE 42

AV INSERT – GE D-6

PPM 30, Lab 30, Con 26, Lib 9

PRESENTER   Up and down the country, PPM leader Joe Newman continues to attract the kind of crowds - both supportive and angrily hostile – that we haven't seen on the streets of Britain since the halcyon days of John Major. His party's poll ratings have now stabilised. Meanwhile three more PPM candidates were expelled from the party today, for expressing extremist views. Mr Newman seems unconcerned. The Conservative Party has now joined Labour and the Liberal Democrats in saying it will not enter into any form of coalition with the PPM.

NIGEL EVANS   The PPM are an absolute disgrace. They are a shambles of a party and they are a blight on British politics. They are the Alf Garnett party of the United Kingdom and I am delighted that our Prime Minister has made it abundantly clear we'll have nothing to do with them.

JOE   This proves, yet again, what a cosy little cartel the established parties have set up between them. If you want a fresh start, if you like what we in the PPM have been saying, you now know what you have to do. You have to vote for us.

SCENE 43

AN OFFICE - GE D-5

PPM 32, Lab 28, Con 25, Lib 10

JOE, SAM and ANNE. They look exhausted, even angry.

ANNE	You have no choice. Our poll lead is just not enough. If you don't give a strong lead now, we are going to lose. It's that simple. All this will have been a total waste of time/
JOE	They've all played into our hands. Colluding against us like this/
SAM	I know. And your response was great, but the polls/
JOE	Oh the bloody polls again.
SAM	Yes, the bloody polls again. Too many people think you've gone weak, that you don't stand for anything.
ANNE	You have to send out a strong, new message. Now. Prove you're capable of leading the nation.
SAM	She's right, Joe, you do have to do something. We have our noses in front again, but we have just five days left to break from the pack.
JOE	So, seriously, what you're suggesting is/
ANNE	Play to your perceived strengths.

SAM	Build on your USP.
ANNE	A clear, concise package of measures to contain and control immigration into this country.
SAM	A harder, clearer line.
ANNE	First, voluntary repatriation.
JOE	Repatriation? Jesus.
ANNE	Voluntary repatriation. We hear all the time that most immigrants want to return home – because a civil war has ended, a famine has been eradicated, they feel homesick, miss their families, whatever.
SAM	Let's give them what they say they want.
ANNE	Islamic preachers should be required to preach in English. Then there's burkas.
JOE	Seriously?
SAM	Where I grew up, we were always warned about men in balaclavas. Men who covered up their faces because they did terrible, brutal things. No face. Just the eyes.
ANNE	We have a long tradition of showing our faces in public. It ought to be respected. If you ride a motorbike, wear a crash helmet. When you get off, you take it off. End of. You have to propose a full ban. Anything less would be/
JOE	Sam and I do things that used to be banned.

ANNE	Don't we know it.
SAM	She'd probably ban them again, given half a chance/
ANNE	So, do you like burkas?
JOE	No I don't, to be honest, no, but me not liking something doesn't justify banning it.
ANNE	Why don't you like them?
JOE	They make me feel uneasy (*beat*). Uncomfortable.
ANNE	Why's that?
JOE	I don't honestly know.
ANNE	Is it because they seem un-British?
JOE	Well, maybe, but...
ANNE	But?
JOE	But they also represent something oppressive. Something medieval. Maybe I'm a feminist.
ANNE	Good. Very good. Then you understand where I'm coming from. Banning these things is a liberal policy.
JOE	Liberal?
ANNE	Tough liberal.

SAM   We're in the last-chance saloon, Joe. You have to rally the troops.

JOE   Alright. Thank you. I just need to think. To think. By myself.

Anne and Sam exit.

SCENE 44

AV INSERT – GE D-4

PPM 32, Lab 30, Con 27, Lib 7

PRESENTER   This has been a remarkable few days for the PPM. Just a week ago it looked dead and buried – and a major part of its problem was its appalling media management. Today brought new drama, when a demonstrator chucked a flour bomb at Mr Newman, who responded by leaving the stage and attacking the man responsible. After he was pulled away from the fracas, Mr Newman said he was sorry, but he wasn't going to apologise.

OBSERVER   This was certainly unorthodox behaviour for someone in the public eye, except a footballer perhaps, but a fresh poll this evening suggests the proportion of voters seeing Mr. Newman as a strong leader has bounced dramatically back up, from 21 to 47 per cent.

JOE   (*Excerpt from speech – also AV*) As Nye Bevan so rightly said, "We could manage to survive without money changers and stockbrokers. We should find it harder to do without miners, steel workers and those who cultivate the land." It is precisely those decent, hard-working, ordinary people whom we, as a nation and as a society, must learn to cherish. My dream is to live in a world, and a country, where we are judged by our fellow citizens not according to our gender or our sexual preferences, our creed or the colour of our skins, but by the quality of our character and the true value of our endeavours.

SCENE 45

GE D-4

JOE & SAM

SAM	So what the Hell was that about?
JOE	Mmmm?
SAM	Nye Bevan. Martin Luther King. It's ridiculous. You should stay on message. Use your script.
JOE	That was my script. My script. And if people don't like it, that's tough.
SAM	If you say so.
JOE	Yes, I do say so. And I'm still the one in charge.
SAM	Joe, we are so close, so close. I can feel it now/
JOE	Feel what, Sam? Power?
SAM	You're no better than I am. You want to be the fairy at the top of the tree, just like I do.
JOE	Maybe, but for very different reasons.

SCENE 46

AV INSERT – GE D-3

PPM 33, Lab 25, Con 27, Lib 10

PRESENTER   Since "Flourbombgate", Joe Newman's personal ratings have bounced back substantially. The PPM too has been enjoying a slight recovery too, with its support creeping back into the mid-30s. Mr Newman continues to draw huge crowds across the country. So it seems to be game on again for the PPM, although experts warn its support is spread so evenly across the country that it has a struggle on its hands if it aims to be the largest grouping in the new House of Commons.

SCENE 47

GE D-2

JOE, ANNE & SAM enter together.

JOE	More packed halls. Still standing Room Only. "SRO".
ANNE	Huge crowds in the streets.
JOE	And people keep throwing things at me. It's very disconcerting.
SAM	One day it's water bombs.
JOE	Then it's eggs.
SAM	Then it's flour.
JOE	They should add a pinch of salt and bake me into a pie.

ANNE's mobile rings. JOE channel hops until he finds himself.

INTERVIEWER	*(On screen)* So, with three days to go, are you feeling confident?
JOE	*(On screen)* This nation – our nation – needs a clear and decisive result. And only the PPM can deliver that.

SAM is looking at his mobile phone. JOE turns the TV off.

	Labour say we'll bugger up the economy. Bloody cheek. They're fine ones to talk/
SAM	Shush. There's been an explosion.

JOE	Where?
SAM	Central London.

ANNE's phone rings.

ANNE	Hello? Yes. Yes, I am with him. (*Beat*). I'll tell him at once. Thank you. Hold on, please.
JOE	Where in Central London? What's going on?

More cacophony of rings and vibrations.

ANNE	Sorry. What were you saying? Jesus, Joe, it was in your flat. No, in your block.
JOE	Was anyone hurt? Was Liz there? Is Liz OK? I have to call her. If she's been hurt/
SAM	(*Very calm & focused*) Joe. Joe. Calm down. Go out there and make the speech. There's nothing you can do just now. We'll find out what's going on.
JOE	Check on Liz. Now. Please.
ANNE	We'll call straight away.
SAM	Deep breaths, Joe, deep breaths.
JOE	Who'd do a thing like this? Oh God. Not that bastard with his bollocks shit placards about badgers? That crazy manifesto. It must be him/
SAM	We'll find out. Now you have to/
JOE	I can't. Liz/

159

SAM   Joe. You have to go out there and speak. I'm sorry. You must.

ANNE and SAM exchange a glance.

SCENE 48

AV – GE D-2

PPM 34, Lab 25, Con 28, Lib 9

OBSERVER   The national campaign by Joe Newman and the Popular People's Movement seems to be in disarray again. Mr Newman's keynote speech today was billed as a great relaunch, with tough new policies on immigration and law and order, but he appeared unsettled or even upset and changed direction entirely as he spoke.

SCENE 49

GE D-2

JOE takes an envelope out of his jacket pocket and reads from the piece of paper within. He moves into the limelight.

JOE Yes, I do believe we must defend our borders and our culture. I make no apology for that. As a wise woman once said, 'let us cherish our own way of life'. It is our right and our responsibility to ourselves and those who follow. And it is only good manners for newcomers to respect our ways. But what is more intrinsic or more precious in our cherished way of life, than our tradition of gentleness, hospitality and the kindness to strangers? There must be no room in our country or our culture for intolerance, for anger or for hatred. So let us not condemn our fellow human beings for seeking safe refuge here.

This is God's own country, so of course people will come. We cannot accept them all as neighbours, but we should respect them as human beings. Before we clamour against them, should we not consider what it must be like, being in their shoes?
"Why, you must needs be strangers.
Would you be pleased
To find a nation of such barbarous

162

temper,
That, breaking out in hideous
violence,
Would not afford you an abode on
earth?"

SCENE 50

AV – GE D-1

PRESENTER/REPORTER   First thing this morning, PPM leader Joe Newman dramatically cancelled all his public campaigning engagements.

ANNE   Mr. Newman had been enjoying the campaign very much, but, in the circumstances, he has decided to suspend his personal campaigning.

PRESENTER/REPORTER   Four hours later, Mr Newman resumed campaigning, after a private visit to friends and neighbours who were injured in yesterday's terrorist attack on his London flat.

SCENE 51

GE D-1

SAM   He's insistent?

ANNE   Absolutely. He'll carry on campaigning, but we're to make no comment at all about the bombing, until the polls have closed.

SAM   But don't you see what an opportunity we've missed?

ANNE   I'm sorry?

SAM   To go really tough. Pledge to clamp down hard, make sure this kind of thing never happens again/

ANNE   Are you being serious?

SAM   You of all people should understand/

ANNE   I of all people?

SAM   He ought to be telling everyone what a terrible blow this is to him, but he's carrying on regardless, in the national interest/

ANNE   You think he should be wringing his hands on television, milking this terrible thing for all it's worth? You really are a bastard.

SAM   Everything else in my life has been a total Horlicks, but I really, really believed this was my chance. Fuck it. Fucking fuck it.

ANNE   I think Liz is paying a much higher price.

SAM   Those fucking stupid bastards couldn't even
                  hit the right flat with their stupid bomb.

SCENE 52

AV – GE D-DAY

PRESENTER   Polls have now closed in what many are calling the most important general election – and certainly the most unpredictable general election – in a generation. The first results, from two very different seats, Sunderland, and Guildford, should be in by 11pm...

SCENE 53

A hospital waiting room. JOE is sitting alone, watching the television screen.

PRESENTER   ...and the new Cabinet will have its first meeting tomorrow morning. In other news, a man aged 56 has been remanded in custody, charged with attempted murder, in connection with the bombing of a flat in London two days before the general election. James Arthur Stanton, of Basildon in Essex...

After a time there is a knock on the door. JOE ignores it. Then a second knock, still quiet, but slightly more insistent. Beat. SAM enters, looking embarrassed and uneasy. JOE turns off the television.

SAM   The press are waiting outside. You're running late.

JOE   Hmmm?

SAM   The press.

JOE   Ha, yes, the press.

SAM   They're waiting for you.

JOE   The press wait for no man? Well they can wait for me. (*Beat*). Sam, there's something I need to discuss with you.

SAM   Right. (*Beat*). OK. Now?

JOE   No, not now. After I've dealt with the press.

SAM	Oh. OK. (*Beat*). I've done a speaking note for you/
JOE	I know what to say.

On his way out, SAM passes MAGGIE. She is walking awkwardly, using a stick.

MAGGIE	Thank you for allowing me in.
JOE	Of course. Thank you for coming.
MAGGIE	I hear the police have made an arrest. Was it your badger man?
JOE	No. (*Beat*). No, it wasn't.
MAGGIE	Well, who was it then? I thought you were certain it/
JOE	I was. And I was wrong. It was a PPM activist.
MAGGIE	What?
JOE	Someone who'd actually been out campaigning for us in the early days. Almost became a candidate.
MAGGIE	I don't know what to say.
JOE	He had a long history of extremist activism. National Front, BNP, UKIP, PPM. Far right, Maggie. Far right. What the fuck was he even thinking of, joining a party that I… (*Beat*). Apparently he thought I was betraying the cause.

169

MAGGIE	His cause?
JOE	The noble cause of England for the English. All White on the Night. Well I bloody well hope I was betraying it.
MAGGIE	He sounds like a right-wing nutter, straight out of central casting.
JOE	It was my fault, all my fault. I can't, I can't/
MAGGIE	It's no good you punishing yourself, as Liz would be the first to tell you. Events/
JOE	Events, dear boy/
MAGGIE	Events acquire their own momentum.
JOE	I couldn't just stop campaigning. I couldn't let everyone down. You do understand?
MAGGIE	Of course I do. And I respect you for not exploiting/
JOE	Really my place should be here. Here is what matters. Liz. Energetic Liz. Funny Liz. Impossible Liz. Liz who's always been there for me, who'll always be there. You should see her now.
MAGGIE	Joe, I'm so, so sorry.
JOE	She didn't even believe in what I was doing. She tried to talk me out of it. She warned me. Then they hurt her because of me.
MAGGIE	What are the doctors saying?

JOE	At first no one would tell me anything. No one would let me know the true facts, how bad things are. Now I wish I hadn't asked.
MAGGIE	And how bad is it?
JOE	She may never recover consciousness. She may be in a coma for the rest of her life.

MAGGIE holds JOE's hand for a moment.

MAGGIE	Can I get you/
JOE	A cup of tea, perhaps?

They smile, gently.

MAGGIE	Of course. The universal panacea to whatever ails an Englishman.
JOE	If only that were true. Thank you.

MAGGIE leaves.

Oh Liz. (*Tiny beat*). Stay for me:

Where souls do couch on flowers,
we'll hand in hand,
And with our sprightly port make
the ghosts... make the ghosts...
gays.

JOSH enters.

JOSH	I'm so sorry, but/
JOE	I know, I know.

JOE stands up, brushes himself down.

JOSH   Do her proud.

JOE   I'll certainly do my best.

They move to leave, JOE moving ahead of JOSH.

JOSH   Good luck, Joe. (*Tiny beat*). Hey, good luck,
                 Prime Minister.

Exeunt. As the stage lights fade slowly, the Screen springs back into life. We see JOE, acknowledging a cheering crowd. The ticker-tape at the bottom of the screen reads: "Joe Newman is new Prime Minister, leading Government of National Unity. PPM dissolved with immediate effect. The new PM pledges to 'govern with humility, humanity and generosity, for the many and not the few...'

THE END